T0149350

The Power of Women in our Sixties

Chris Vidal

BALBOA
PRESS

A DIVISION OF HAY HOUSE

Copyright © 2019 Chris Vidal.

All rights reserved. No part of this book may be used or reproduced by any means, graphic, electronic, or mechanical, including photocopying, recording, taping or by any information storage retrieval system without the written permission of the author except in the case of brief quotations embodied in critical articles and reviews.

Balboa Press books may be ordered through booksellers or by contacting:

Balboa Press
A Division of Hay House
1663 Liberty Drive
Bloomington, IN 47403
www.balboapress.com.au
1 (877) 407-4847

Because of the dynamic nature of the Internet, any web addresses or links contained in this book may have changed since publication and may no longer be valid. The views expressed in this work are solely those of the author and do not necessarily reflect the views of the publisher, and the publisher hereby disclaims any responsibility for them.

The author of this book does not dispense medical advice or prescribe the use of any technique as a form of treatment for physical, emotional, or medical problems without the advice of a physician, either directly or indirectly. The intent of the author is only to offer information of a general nature to help you in your quest for emotional and spiritual well-being. In the event you use any of the information in this book for yourself, which is your constitutional right, the author and the publisher assume no responsibility for your actions.

Any people depicted in stock imagery provided by Getty and Adobe Images are models, and such images are being used for illustrative purposes only.
Certain stock imagery © Getty Images.

Print information available on the last page.

ISBN: 978-1-5043-1830-3 (sc)
ISBN: 978-1-5043-1833-4 (e)

Balboa Press rev. date: 08/26/2019

CONTENTS

ACKNOWLEDGEMENTS

I love working with like-minded women who have similar values. I am immensely grateful to Kathy Knott, a kindred spirit, who took on the challenge of working with me over several months to turn my first rough draft of this book into something I am proud of. Without this encouragement, editing and writing skills, this book may never have come to fruition. You retained my voice in these pages Kathy, yet had the expertise to lift my game. Thank you.

My daughter Nicole and son Ryan have always backed me with their enthusiasm and dedication, and I am endlessly proud of them. My Mum has been a rock, always there for me, and I love her wise words, coming to me at just the right time!

My precious friends and the women who gather in the Meetup groups I organise, are all so inspiring, I thank them for sharing their stories of inspiration, struggle and determination with openness and good humour. It is always a pleasure to be in their company, as every woman in their sixties has a story to tell!

Thank you all.
Chris

INTRODUCTION

This is the best time ever for women in our sixties. If we use it wisely, this decade between our responsible fifties and our relaxed seventies offers us a once-in-a-lifetime opportunity to reinvent ourselves and start something new, on our own terms. We can learn new skills, make new friends and connections, have adventures, make a difference, create a new personal style, and meet other fabulous women our age, all with a story to tell.

Sadly though, many women have a negative attitude towards this time of their life, due to early conditioning and cultural biases around ageing. They may think life will be all downhill from sixty; or they live in denial, withdrawn or lacking confidence, instead of looking forward to their sixties as an exciting time rich with potential.

Among my many interests and activities, I manage a Meetup group with 500 members (and rising), called 'The Power of Women in Our Sixties', based in the Gold Coast in Australia. When I floated the concept of a book like this one to inspire and empower women in their sixties, the reaction of members was overwhelmingly positive, so I decided to do it.

By writing this book I hope to reach out to you and galvanise you to take firm control of your life in the decade ahead. I want to show you that you have the power to decide who you want to be, where you want to go, and what you want to accomplish. And you *can* make any changes that are important to you.

We can seek and find the peace, fulfillment and inner contentment that possibly escaped us during our working or younger years. More than that – we have the right to. The joys of grandparenting and strengthening family connections can also add a new and meaningful dimension to our lives.

This book has taken a while to write, it has been my companion! My original ideas, which I explored in my late 50s, changed somewhat as I explored the extraordinary potential in this new decade I was approaching. As I delved further, a saw a new exciting future bursting with opportunities open up – if I dared seize it. The realisation that this decade presents a unique chance to take control of the rest of my life was both thrilling and liberating.

And so it became my mission to share this excitement with other women like you, also in or near your sixties. As you read this book you will see why it is imperative that you don't keep it to yourself! I encourage you to share it with your friends, family, husband, partner, and other significant people. Their support and understanding will help you achieve your sixties' goals, and must not be understated. And who knows, they may be inspired to join you on your journey and transform and enrich their own lives as well as yours.

There are so many opportunities out there waiting for us. As I write this book I am discovering them for myself as well, and I want to share them with you. Have the courage to join me on this amazing path – and read on!

CHAPTER 1

The Best Time Ever to be Sixty

If you are a woman in your sixties, living in a democratic and developed country as I do, you will know we are unbelievably fortunate compared to many of our sisters who fight for survival in undeveloped countries torn apart by war, religion or politics.

We privileged sixty-year-old women have a decade ahead of us to reinvent ourselves; exciting years to do anything we choose that reaffirms our life's values and purpose. Far from being 'over the hill' or past our 'use-by date', many women feel relief at reaching this stage of life, which Jane Fonda calls our 'Third Act'. It is a time to indulge in the finer things in life: time, comfort, interest and friendships. We can start something new, learn a new skill, create new connections to make a difference, develop a new personal style and meet other fabulous sixty year old women - all who have a story to tell!

Interestingly, research published by Bankwest in 2013 and 2015 found that Australian women aged over 65 are starting their own businesses at a rate unmatched by any other generation in the last 10 years. The NBN™ Silver Economy Report in 2017 confirmed this trend.

I understand that it's natural to feel negative or depressed about turning sixty. Many sad stories remind me of the fragility of life and give me food for thought about this decade. But instead of being full of trepidation, I'm full of anticipation and excitement, as I'm the one in control. I have choices. I believe that our sixties are a gift, a chance to do things we have always wanted to do, so let's pile a whole load of happiness and adventure in there.

The old saying 'life is what you make it' is true for most of us. If we believe this, then surely we should feel privileged and have a conscious desire to do something worthwhile with this opportunity.

I do understand though that many women, burdened with life's struggles or unfortunate circumstances, may not yet be in a position at this stage of their lives to take full advantage of this privilege. Some of these women tell me the most incredible life stories. Facing overwhelming challenges, they bravely soldier on to make the most of their lives and retain hope for a better future. Human beings are never guaranteed a lengthy or uncomplicated life, and for those of us lucky enough to be able to control our destinies, how we choose to experience this decade is up to us.

Think back to your twenties and thirties. Like most of us, you were probably too preoccupied with study, finding the right job, relationships, and probably babies, to think about the distant future. At times we were flippant and carefree, and possibly naively irresponsible in our judgment or decision-making. If we wanted to try something, we just did it – probably with far less money than we have now.

I believe we can be more liberated now in our sixties than we were in the feisty 1970s, in the heady early days of women's liberation. Consider the vast changes in our world since then – attitudes, developments, inventions, perceptions and discoveries of every sort. The facilities in our homes would dazzle our grandmothers!

What if we push ourselves outside our comfort zones and discover we have a talent for something we have never thought of? What is stopping us? As sixty-something women, how lucky we are to be living at this time.

When we were growing up, nobody told us that life events could unexpectedly tear us apart, or that unforeseen health issues might test us physically and emotionally. We were sheltered from that – if we were lucky.

Change, though, is inevitable: it can happen without warning and alter the direction of our lives in dramatic and sometimes traumatic ways.

> *Karen was married and in her early thirties when her life was abruptly shattered after her one-year-old daughter emptied her father's briefcase onto the floor. Oops … papers went everywhere, so mum and daughter gathered them up. Karen noticed an envelope addressed to a woman in her husband's handwriting. With a sickening feeling and racing heart, she opened it. It was a love letter – and in an instant her life changed. Devastated and with emotions out of control, she felt she'd been belted with a bat.*
>
> *This unexpected turn of events eventually forced her to make some huge decisions – stay or not stay? Once trust had been broken she felt unsure and anchorless, and eventually divorced her husband. Although time*

Life isn't about finding yourself.
Life is about creating yourself!

—Unknown

heals most things, as it did for Karen, it took raw courage to start out on her own Plan B and follow a different path.

You are never too old to set another goal or to dream a new dream.

—Unknown

By our sixties we know that unexpected change happens at any time, and that it is inevitable. So instead of waiting for it to knock on our door, why not create exciting and interesting experiences that equip us to cope with these challenges? Compared to our younger, more innocent selves, we are now stronger and hopefully wiser. We should know ourselves well by now, and this decade might be our last real chance to start something that is enduring and amazing, and reflects who we are.

For sure, we can't all take a leap into the unknown and guarantee success – but let's ask 'Why not?' and open our minds to the possibilities that emerge. Rather than let our sixty-plus years of experience, knowledge and wisdom become stagnant or wasted, let's see what happens when we say 'Yes I can'.

We must act now because – let's face it – it may be our last serious chance to create a new and rewarding future. No-one likes to confront the inevitable downside of becoming older and forgetful! Like me, you probably find remembering passwords, codes, account numbers, your glasses, wallets and car keys exhausting.

As for our bodies – we need all the help we can get to look after this precious commodity so it hums during the decades ahead. Let's regard our body as our temple that has served us well for sixty years. It has woken each morning and performed well, coped with our diet fads, over-indulgences, extremes and shortcomings. Consider what's inside this temple – our major organs including heart, lungs, intestines, stomach and kidneys – all serving a vital purpose.

So much is constantly being discovered about longevity and ageing; there are more centenarians than ever in the world today, with the numbers continuing to grow. Genetic testing can predict what disease or illness we may be susceptible to, and routine testing can pick up disease before it takes hold in our bodies. Advances in surgical procedures and rehabilitation programs mean we recover more quickly after medical events. Natural therapies and preventatives abound. So if we look after our bodies in our sixties, they may also give us little or no pain well into our seventies.

At age forty-nine I knew the big five-0 was looming, but I was in denial; when my daughter asked me how I wanted to celebrate I was fairly negative. I didn't feel fifty; I didn't want to be fifty; and I did not want to celebrate being fifty! It had just snuck up and I wasn't ready for it. After complaining to an older work colleague she said, 'For goodness sake, just celebrate that you are still alive and healthy!' I was stunned – but of course she was right! So I changed my mindset: my daughter organised a great celebration and I had a fantastic birthday. My motto since then has been: *Never miss an opportunity!*

"Most people miss great opportunities because of their misperception of time. Don't wait! The time will never be just right."

—Stephen C Hogan

Everyone has their own unique idea of what happiness is for them, and we need to understand that no-one else can make us happy. It's our responsibility, our choice, and ultimately our pleasure. For me, happiness is waking up each morning, eager and excited about the possibilities ahead.

Each week, I drive to my work in another city, stay a few nights, then return home. Most people dread this stressful journey as the traffic is horrendous, as it is in most big cities. To change my experience, I decided this is my time and I organise it accordingly. I sing along to my favourite music; read magazines during any traffic jams; slather on body lotion when I can, and enjoy my favourite aromatherapy essence to calm my senses. It's my time with just me on the road with time to think, assess and plan. I often glance at other drivers and imagine their life, what it's about, where they are heading, and whether they are happy.

Different stages of life present us with different choices. When we were young there was little or no forward planning: life was for living in the moment, and most of the time we ran by the seat of our pants. We lived life spontaneously, always in the present, and with little planning for the future. Then came careers, long-term relationships, often children, mortgages, commitments – generally taking things seriously and figuring life out.

In our sixties, however, we are generally free of other obligations and can plan in order to make the most of this decade of choices.

As you read this book I want you to take these questions seriously and figure out your responses:

- How do I want to spend my sixties?
- What exciting possibilities are available to me?
- What have I never done, and really want to try?
- What can I accomplish?
- Is this something that could put zest into my life?
- Is the possibility a reality?

Think about each question and consider how you will feel if you do nothing new; if where you are is where you stay; and if you never explore the possibilities out there for the taking.

I've had the best life so far and I would not change a thing. I learned early that if Plan A didn't eventuate, I could put Plan B in place. I'm now way down the alphabet in plans; however the journeys have been fun and engaging, and have helped me appreciate family, friends and good people along the way.

I was a school teacher for fifteen years, then I made a change. I had nine jobs in the next twenty years and I've had a real ball accomplishing things I never thought possible. People have asked me: 'Chris, shouldn't you deal with your issue of moving from job to job?' to which I have replied: 'What – and miss an opportunity?'

Throughout my chopping and changing career I have met some incredible people who have opened up opportunities, friendships and challenges along the way.

Now I'm in my sixties, I am loving looking ahead and deciding what I want in this decade. I know full-heartedly that it has to include happiness, good health, meeting interesting people, and feeling fulfilled.

Our lives are a collection of the stories we create. One of my special ones, that I often recall, dates back twenty years when I spent a large part of my life in Singapore. A close friend and I had our babies close together, and years later, babies now in their early teens, it was time for us to go our separate ways. I was shocked when my friend suggested that we both get a tattoo to reflect our long and close friendship. But, in the spirit of the relationship, I did it!

Having a bamboo pattern tattooed on my ankle, while she had a flower bracelet inked on her wrist, was the most painful thing I have ever done, but to this day we still laugh about it, and I have related the story so many times. Now, in my sixties, I look back and thank my dear friend for suggesting something so crazy.

I believe we need to continue creating new stories in our sixties – ones that will either surprise us with delight or shock us with possibilities.

At the Power of Women in our Sixties Meet Up groups which I organise, I ask the question: 'And who are you?' This simple question elicits some fascinating, inspiring and sometimes very sad life stories.

Jackie, a fairly serious and somewhat sad-looking lady arrived. She was well built, short dark hair and obviously not confident within herself. She looked a little nervous and wasn't open to making conversation with other women. I always feel empathy for the quiet, reserved person presuming that they may have had a difficult life. After settling down and ordering our coffees we listened to some fascinating life stories and finally came to Jackie. I couldn't believe how the body language changed as Jackie said with a big smile: 'I'm Jackie and so pleased to be here. I'm an ex-racing driver and I've had the most wonderful life'. We all gasped as she went on to tell her story of how as young girl she had wanted to drive fast cars and feel the thrill of action, competition and winning. Since then she has come to many meetings and instead of sitting reserved and quiet, she has been fiery and eager to socialise with us all.

Stories don't just happen – you have to get out there and live life to its fullest: meet new people; travel and surround yourself with people who feed you happiness; help others in need; have adventures; sit and take in the wonder.

You are being presented
with a choice:
Evolve or remain.
If you choose to remain unchanged,
you will be presented with
the same challenges,
the same routine, the same
storms, the same situations,
until you learn from them,
until you choose change.
If you choose to evolve,
you will connect with the
strength within you.

—Creig Crippen

CHAPTER 2

Qualification of Power

So how do we sixty year olds define 'The Power of a Sixty Year Old Woman'? 'Power' is a very strong word yet I deliberately choose to use it. I don't mean power based on rank, physical strength or influence.

We are powerful women. We have experienced this world for sixty-plus years, and tried and tested a lot of things. We have been babies, had babies, raised children, and become grandparents.

We have been teenagers, studied for a career, attended interviews (successful or otherwise), learned how to hold down a job, worked with inspiring or dreadful co-workers, fallen in love and out of it, been jealous, envious, let down, fired, or dumped many times.

We have been mothers, wives, daughters, partners and carers. We have experienced many jobs whilst raising a family, and supported the community with voluntary work. We have cared for others who were unwell while unwell ourselves – and still carried on.

Friends have come in and out of our lives and we continue to grow older gracefully, intelligently, and with a willingness to learn more about ourselves. Hopefully we have also learned to handle our money, health and emotions.

That's real power!

Be the kind of woman
that when your feet
hit the floor
each morning
the devil says
·OH CRAP, SHE'S UP!·

—Unknown

The world today is very different from when I was a teenager living in a closeted and safe world. I was conditioned to follow what adults said and did without question. We were so self-conscious then – concerned if our bra straps showed or if our stockings or tights had ladders and holes. Were our skirts too short and did our colours (and lipsticks) match in every way?

We have come a long way since then and now at our age we can wear coloured bras to match our outfit if we choose, and feel happy for them to be seen!

When I was growing up, subjects such as periods, sex, boys and relationships seemed to be taboo and were seldom mentioned. We only learned about these things from friends who were more open. At boarding school, after lights out, we had Friday night chats on a chosen bed in the dormitory. I was horrified at first to learn of such personal things, but soon I became the one who shared the information with new boarders. Our mums never had discussions with their mums, so it was left to us to find out about our periods, sex, relationships, and even pregnancy.

I remember when one of our popular women's magazines openly discussed periods for the first time. Later, in the early 1970s, the Australian magazine *Cleo*, under the stewardship of a young Ita Buttrose, produced a controversial sealed section containing 'explicit and mature content' such as orgasms, breast size, sexual habits and libido. *Cleo* also brought us the first nude male centerfolds. We eagerly bought the magazine, ripped open the sealed section and read the contents with shock and surprise, taking care to hide it later. (Ita, Australian women thank you!)

As young women, I think we did extremely well considering the cultural changes we lived through, the gender expectations that often limited us, the intolerance for difference that surrounded us, and the emotions that were often overwhelming, unexplained and ignored!

We managed without access to the information and support that is available now. Growing up, we took chances, picked ourselves up after being dumped, and struggled through family crises. After becoming mothers, we gave of ourselves totally, watching our children develop whilst we stayed still, and eventually let them go. Our power has grown from this vast experience – and we must acknowledge and congratulate ourselves for decades of nurturing and learning, as well as our successes and failures.

Nothing today seems taboo, and yet I believe we sixty-year-olds have mostly maintained our self-pride, dignity and decorum, which has resulted from our more conservative upbringing in a different age. Hopefully we have moved with the times too.

> At another meeting when her turn came around, Alison started to speak rather timidly and I certainly didn't expect anything as extraordinary as her story. She came to Australia from New

"A woman is like a tea bag.
You never know
how strong she is
until she gets in hot water."

—Eleanor Roosevelt

Zealand in her early thirties and after working in Sydney she joined a charity and was sent off to the northern parts of Vietnam, working in an orphanage for young girls whose mothers had fallen pregnant to American soldiers during the war. These women could not afford to bring up their daughters so many were left out in fields. The helicopter pilots would fly over mountainous terrain rescuing these little girls to bring them to the orphanage. After a few months one of the pilots suggested to Alison that it would be a huge help if she got her flying licence as they were struggling to cope with the numbers of girls - so she did! For a couple of years Alison helped rescue the little girls from mountainous regions. The emotions and basic hard work of living in Vietnam was enough but on top of that navigating a helicopter through the steep terrain hillsides must have been terrifying.

Are you going to let all of your valuable experiences fade into nothing? No! You have a real opportunity to use and develop your power to make your sixties something extraordinary. If you don't believe that all the years before have been of value, then what were they for? If you take the time to look at each decade and write down your achievements and failures, you can see you did a hell of a lot!

Always remember
you are BRAVER
Than you believe
STRONGER
Than you seem
SMARTER
Than you think

—A. A. Milne

Think back to your years of education. How many years did you spend training for a career? I spent three years at teachers training college studying for my primary school teaching certificate then taught for 15 years. If you have never been a teacher and aspire to, you can now become one in less than three years! Or you can gain a qualification to be an art or music teacher, a first aid teacher, an IT creative, even a dance teacher (quick, before you can't move so easily!). The opportunities are waiting.

Kathy gained a master's degree one month before she turned sixty, showing that it's never too late to learn. When she attended her first Meetup event with my group, The Power of 60 Year Old Women, she talked about growing up in New Zealand in the 60s and 70s. Most girls then were expected to become mothers and housewives, filling in their time after leaving school with teaching, nursing or secretarial work. She fulfilled the early motherhood and teaching roles, then after her marriage broke up she was determined to make something of her life and abilities for herself and two daughters. She changed direction and through hard work and dedication she rose to the top of her field in marketing and public relations, travelling around the world. In her fifties she decided to attend university while also working full-time. Five years later, a month before her sixtieth, she graduated with a Master of Business, also winning the Dean's Award for Excellence, as well as four academic prizes. A summary of her thesis was published in an international academic journal.

Some of you may have studied for years like Kathy; others may never have used your training; and many will have had amazing careers resulting from dedication and hard work. I am adamant that you are living in the best time to be sixty, with more potential available to you than ever before. If you start something new each month for twelve months, and stick at it each day, studies show that you could be well-trained and knowledgeable in twelve new experiences.

For example, you could learn to:

- Play an unusual instrument
- Dance – any style that suits you

- Sing, solo or in a choir
- Become knowledgeable about the stock market
- Enjoy gardening or flower decorating
- Practice yoga, Pilates, meditation classes
- Embroider, knit or make quilts
- Debate or speak publicly, through Toastmasters
- Evaluate and appraise antiques
- Critique literature
- Take better photographs from the Internet
- Study psychology
- Become a curator in an art gallery or museum
- Fundraise for a charity
- Create an artwork or dabble for fun
- Do anything of your choice!

So let's consider – are these things really possible? When you turn sixty you have ten years ahead of you, ten full years – and then some more – to enjoy. Why not give things a go? It's not about success or failure: the benefits of reinventing yourself now will flow into your seventies and beyond. Hopefully you still have vitality, a positive mindset and an able body to serve you well through this decade and into the next, with good energy. But if you view the decade negatively, it will all seem a long stretch of time with little fulfillment.

The only way to use your power is to take action and decide how to move forward. I have become passionate about the opportunities I see around me, and I believe that we will all be more successful if we collaborate with other successful, like-minded and determined women.

When I tell women that I'm writing a book entitled 'The Power of Women in Their Sixties …', their reply is more often than not: 'Oh, I will read that. I so need some motivation.'

I invite you to create your own sixties partnership with me on this journey. Read on to discover the possibilities.

When women support each other, incredible things happen.

—Unknown

CHAPTER 3

My Circle of Life

During twenty-two years of primary school teaching, I learned the basics of life coaching, and it is this: If you make a child feel good about themselves, they can achieve almost anything.

While living and working in Indonesia, Singapore, Sri Lanka and Australia, I listened to many young women who needed reassurance that they were valued and on the right track. By listening and allowing them to express themselves, they recognised their self-worth.

I joined the Australian Life Coaching Academy and I learned another important thing – that we all talk too much! We are born with two ears and one mouth for a good reason, and we learn so much about others from listening. I believe that due to our vast life experience, listening is something we sixty-year-olds do exceptionally well. Let's use this skill to listen and guide the younger generation, and help them feel good about themselves. We don't need a psychology degree, just two ears to listen and a caring heart to encourage.

A question I ask my life coaching clients to elicit a powerful response is this: 'What do you love about yourself?' – and they usually then struggle uncomfortably to find an answer. I believe this is because we are all too busy, or modest, to recognise our strengths and successes. We don't do ourselves justice by not acknowledging our own achievements, or by envying others, wishing to be like them, and thinking we are not good enough.

Reviewing and examining the sixty or more years we have lived is a powerful way of realising how fulfilling our lives have actually been. Think about the most rewarding aspects of your life – not just the big things, but the small things, people, relationships and journeys you have experienced. Regardless of where you were born or where you lived, the decisions and paths you chose were unique because we are all unique. All of us have been tested along the way with difficult relationships, health issues and life's disappointments. That's just the human condition.

I liken life to the game of Snakes & Ladders, starting from zero and moving up to one hundred, with the snakes and ladders of life scattered randomly (or not) along the journey. For sure, life is no fairy tale of ladders, and the snakes are always waiting to test us. Have you been strong enough to overcome the snakes, to persevere and climb the next ladder? Bravo! This book will equip you with even more useful tools!

I have also developed an excellent technique to help you identify and validate your achievements. My Circle of Life exercise is a simple, fun and creative way to review your life and appreciate your worth right now. You simply create a life picture that shows just how jam-packed with rich experiences, adventures, opportunities and decisions your life has been so far.

I have facilitated this exercise with many groups of women, and the insights they gain are incredible. I invite you to do this exercise right now, because you will find so much more value in this book if you do.

You will need:

- A piece of A4 paper
- A side plate (to fit within the paper)
- A pencil/colouring pencils/crayons/felt pens/ pens

Steps:

- Place the plate upside down in the middle of the paper and draw around it. Landscape or portrait orientation, it doesn't matter.
- Write your heading 'My Circle of Life' either top left or right and your signature at bottom left or right – creatively as you would a piece of art.

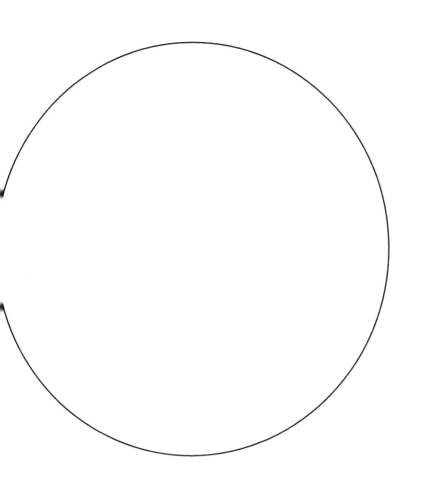

My Circle of Life
by Chris Vidal

Give yourself half an hour to an hour for this exercise, and see what happens.

Close your eyes and relax. Take your mind up to a cloud and sit on it. Look down and think of all the people, events, celebrations, hurdles, dramas, challenges, adventures and laughs that have contributed to your life. Let them come into focus, and observe rather than react.

Enjoy the process. You will draw, doodle, write, create – express everything and anything that comes to mind. (I hear two different reactions to this exercise: the circle is too big, or the circle is too small!)

- Creatively write your name in the middle of the circle.
- Within the circle write down all the countries you have visited in your lifetime.
- How many romantic relationships have you had? Can you remember their names?
- Who is in your extended family? Write down as many names as you can.
- How many homes have you lived in?
- How many years of education have you had? (Start with 8 years of formal schooling)
- How many jobs have you had? What were they?
- What illnesses have you had?
- Name your closest girlfriends
- List your interests/hobbies throughout your life
- How many cars have you owned? Can you name the brands?
- Which successful/unsuccessful diets have you tried?

- How many times have you won something and what were they?
- How many holidays have you had? Where?
- Write down a list of your favourite pieces of clothing over the years. (Mine would have to be a denim skirt, sarong dress)
- Write down as many adventures you can remember throughout your life that come to mind and just let them roll out.

When you are done – or when the circle is full, whichever comes first - sit back and read through it:

- How do you feel about this right now?
- What are your greatest achievements so far?
- What would you change?
- What would you like to have another go at?
- Where are the crossroads – when would you have chosen another direction?
- Any regrets?
- People you admire – why?
- What did you consider unfair?
- How do you view yourself in the bigger world?
- What have you completely finished with?
- Who do you think values you?
- What are your best qualities?
- What's missing?

What is within the circle is everything you have experienced and accomplished up to now. However, there is so much more to do and this is what your sixties decade is for!

Next, look at your Circle of Life and highlight or underline the things you have not completed, or want to progress. Are there countries you want to re-visit, people you wish to see, relationships you want to develop and hobbies to pursue? Or maybe purchase another car or move home? These are exciting prospects.

Next, draw a line from those things inside the circle to the outside. These will show all the things you want to achieve during your sixties. By now you will have many possibilities and plans spilling out of the circle. No time to waste: start planning!

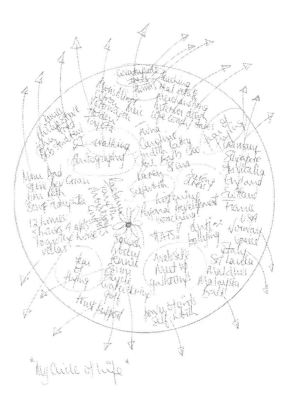

"My Circle of Life"

Life is a circle of happiness,
sadness, hard times
and good times.
If you are going through
Hard times have faith
That good times are
On the way.

—www.livelifehappy.com

Now, looking at all of the things outside the circle, think about:

- What is your top priority?
- What would you like to learn from scratch?
- You have a month to live, how will you spend it?
- What are your biggest fears?
- What excites you?
- If you won $20million, how would it change you?
- How would you like to be remembered?
- What's missing?

This exercise shows that your Circle of Life can be expanded to achieve so much more. As women in our fifties and sixties, we have the experience and now the maturity to forge ahead!

It was a terrible shock for Jennifer to be diagnosed with breast cancer in her early sixties. Sick, with her energy sapped from the treatment, she tried to adjust to the reality of her situation, but often sank into despair, fearfully thinking about her future. Being a strong-minded lady, she wrote down the pros and cons of a number of possibilities. She didn't know how her illness would control her life but could she take some control of it? Not knowing how long she might have, Jennifer decided to live life to the full. She bought a campervan and travelled around beautiful parts of Australia. A few years and thousands of kilometers later, she rests and recuperates at home in between adventures.

CHAPTER 4

Attitude

Our sixties are all about attitude and mindset. Preparing for an adventure or a project at any stage of life is essential to its outcome. Getting the most out of this amazing time in our lives requires a clear focus, with deliberate intention. We need to fire up our attitude, and plan to make things happen. Imagine the fun!

You have ten years or less ahead of you in your sixties decade – and the clock starts now! Rather than see that as a negative, choose a positive attitude and see that the next decade is yours for the taking. This mindset will give you real sense of purpose and excite you with possibilities.

No more tired excuses like 'Oh well, I used to do that' or 'I'm too old now'. Re-boot your thinking and ask 'Why not?' and 'How would I feel if I never tried?'

Our sixties require a special attitude, so if you don't have one, go get one! Attitude is defined as: 'A way of thinking or feeling about something'. This decade calls for an extra dimension of inner strength, deliberate thought and determined action, to uniquely shape the way we walk, talk, dress and react to people and situations.

How often do you hear, or experience for yourself, that women in their sixties are forgotten, ignored or treated as though they are insignificant? We can feel that people pass us by, that we are taken for granted and made to feel unimportant. I say: Think again! Switch on your attitude and get out there!

Jane Fonda's brilliant TED Talk, *Life's Third Act*, delivered in 2012, is enlightening: you can search for it at www.ted.com. She believes that the most important revolution she is now involved in is the 'longevity revolution' – changing a society stuck in the old paradigm of ageing as a 'decline into decrepitude'.

And then one day
I discovered my own light
My own inner gangster
I snatched my power back
And the game changed

—Unknown

Now in her eighties, Ms Fonda states that we are living beyond the lifespan of our grandparents, in a new dimension of life marked by wisdom and happiness. Like Ms Fonda, let's defy the old paradigm by changing our mindset and our attitude to growing older by exploring the many possibilities available to us in later life. Personally, I'm so excited by life: every day there are possibilities to add something, be it a new friend, an interesting experience, an act of kindness or a new learning.

I met Wilma at one of my Sixties Meetup groups. Sitting at a table in the café, she greeted me with a big smile. After other guests arrived, we all told our story. Wilma was last to speak and was particularly moving. She had been married twice, physically abused and had four children, now grown up. Two had medical issues and two were still living at home. She had a full-time job and now on her own, she was trying to set up her son with a business. Despite her sad life, she was full of determination to make the rest of her life count. When we all got up to leave Wilma said, 'Off you go, I'll take my time.'

I said I'd wait, and it was then I saw her reach for two calipers to assist her in walking. She had had polio as a child. I was shocked and asked her how she coped with everything. 'You know Chris, I'm happy at 60 years of age. I appreciate the little things and have some great friends.' She got into her car and drove off … what an attitude!

What you think of yourself
Is much more important
Than what other people
Think of you!

—Unknown

Our attitude also impacts our success in finding the work that makes us happy, whether that is running our own business or creatively finding a job. We all need enough money to sustain ourselves, in order to lead a fulfilling life without worry. While the aged pension is a privilege in this country, the payments are low, and the eligibility and rules can change at any time, according to politicians' whims.

Historically, lower pay rates for women because of part-time work and time out to have a family, can mean that women's retirement savings are much less than men's. In Australia, various reports show that many women in their fifties and sixties are economically disadvantaged, and single women aged fifty-five and over make up about seventy percent of the homeless. These are sobering findings, which the government has yet to address adequately.

Finding a job can be tough in your sixties if you don't have a recent track record, experience or qualifications. Even if you do, ageism is real and employers are often reluctant to hire older people, although research shows we are more reliable, honest and hardworking.

During an agency interview, I asked if I was amongst the oldest applying for a job. The young lady interviewing me replied, 'Yes I guess so, but at least I know you will turn up!'

Our greatest assets are our values, such as trustworthiness, punctuality and focus, and our life experience, so be proud of them and be unafraid to point them out.

Life is to be lived.
If you have to support
yourself, you had bloody better
find some way that
is going to be
interesting. And you
don't do that
by sitting around.

—Katharine Hepburn

If you need extra income, you will need positive energy and attitude to find it. Although buckets of money help of course, you don't need a huge amount to enjoy some of the simpler things in life. Although some of my suggestions won't make you rich, some creative and practical opportunities to earn money include baby sitting and childcare, reading to children, cleaning, taxi driving or working in a café (a barista training certificate is available online). Also, women in our age group are awesomely efficient in customer service, information centres or as receptionists for business.

When I returned to Australia from Sri Lanka early 2005 I didn't know what to do for work. I had spent two of my three years there in Colombo setting up a furniture business, and the third year working for a jeweller who owned fifteen stores in upmarket resorts in the Maldives, a group of islands to the south-west of Sri Lanka, in the Indian Ocean. I had the most wonderful job, flying to islands by seaplane or travelling by boat to upmarket resorts, restyling the stores and training the staff. Returning to Australia, reality hit hard!

I found it tough to find work so my daughter suggested I drive for an online-based ridesharing company. Hang on, I thought, from an exciting, high-flying job to a taxi driver? Anyway, I did it and it turned into a great job because I made it so, by being extremely helpful to my clients and playing them wonderful music. For three months I met the most interesting people and earnings were good, as I generally worked from 5am through to midday, taking people from the city to the airport. Today you can join *Women who Drive for Women*, and again, you are in control. If a friend wants to meet for coffee, you just pause the business rideshare app!

I now work as a boarding house supervisor (house mum) in a private girls' school and love it! My job is to look after feisty thirteen to seventeen-year-old girls full of energy and emotions, who argue with their parents and often think the educational system is quite irrelevant to their future! They are also very capable: they say what they think and generally love life.

Consider this: if we think we have it tough at sixty, think about young girls who are facing a future filled with very different influences, rules and expectations than we ever had. In the meantime, they study for their ideal job, battle stress, anxiety, and even depression. They are more open to possibilities and non-conformity, and bear more pressure than ever. If you have patience and excellent listening skills, being a boarding house mum is a great job for sixty-year-olds.

Another income opportunity could be to set up your own professional service. With our years of experience, and listening skills, we are perfectly suited to counselling, life coaching, mentoring or similar, and there are many training courses available to us. Many young people are craving for someone to listen to them – no evaluation, no negativity, simply someone to listen so they can talk out loud without fear of judgment.

> I met June, aged 59, at one of my Meetup groups. Full of energy and easy to talk to, she had been on her own for many years and had recently moved north for a warmer climate. When I asked what kept her busy she excitedly replied that she had just found her passion and was turning it into a business. She explained that although she had always been creative, she never took herself seriously. Recently she had discovered an epoxy clay in vibrant colours and had successfully experimented with it. She loved creating necklaces, bracelets and earrings, and was just about ready to exhibit her pieces on a small scale. I

Be thankful for what you have,
You'll end up having more,
If you concentrate on
What you don't have,
You will never ever have enough.

—Oprah Winfrey

thought this was a very daring exercise, but she explained that it was all under control, with her family assisting with setting up a website and helping her with the business side of things. She was so proud that at her age she was having a go – and her new-found energy and interest made her very happy, sparking an attitude that will give her new business the edge it needs!

While I was working for an event planner on the Gold Coast, I met a couple of dynamic ladies in a high-end hotel prior to the annual racing carnival. *Everyone there was dressed up to the nines and I complimented one lady on her glamorous and very upmarket outfit, which consisted of a beautiful floral dress, gorgeous high heel shoes and a sassy hat perched sideways on her head.*

I thought that she must have spent a fortune on her outfit and I summoned up the courage to ask her where she had bought it. Smiling, she whispered that the total cost was $47, purchased from a couple of op shops. 'Wait till you see what my friend's wearing!' she said. When her friend arrived, she looked amazing too!

Both ladies, in their early sixties, were cleaners with their own company, which they had run for twenty years. They enjoyed dressing up for various occasions as the highlight of their year. When cleaning, they dressed in aerobic gear, put on music they loved, chose wonderful houses to clean, and loved their jobs. They had attitude!

Here are another couple of income-generating possibilities. They won't suit everyone, but these examples may open your mind and spark some creative thinking around sources of income.

There are a growing number of ironing companies in most cities, servicing busy working people who deposit their ironing in a hole in the wall – and fabulous modern ironing machinery does the rest. People pay $120 for a basket of ironing, and the business works hard to meet the demand.

I'm sure we can all iron very well at sixty-plus – with a bit of attitude! Turn the music up, pause and exercise your core muscles as you work!

If you have a spare room, you have potential income. I rent a room in my apartment to a professional for $1,000 a month, and this is my travelling budget to visit my family and friends overseas during three months of school holidays each year.

A certain attitude is required to step into something unfamiliar, be it a large room of people, a new Meetup group, or simply to walk out wearing a new outfit. It's about opening your mind to a bigger picture for your life, taking away the pettiness of self-doubt, and developing positive 'self-speak'.

Yet, too often women doubt themselves despite their vast experiences and innate wisdom. I am astounded by the remarkable stories and accomplishments of sixty-year-olds which I hear regularly, yet rather than acknowledge their earned status of 'wonder woman', they hold back because of hang ups and self-doubt.

Instead, we should all be holding our heads high with pride.

How can you restore or gain new confidence? There are many motivational courses, presentations and group discussions to be found online, at the local library or in women's groups. The volume of easy to access life-enhancing publications in print and online is vast and limitless. Young people use these tools to build their confidence in life, and you too can take advantage of them to create a new focus – especially if you have been limited or damaged by early criticism or negative experiences.

> *Ruth, aged 65, told our Meetup group about her search for a job. Divorced and living with one of her four children, she desperately wanted to be financially independent. She shared with us her past high-level corporate*

Six months from now
you can be in a completely
different space, mentally,
spiritually & financially.
Keep working and believing
in yourself.

responsibilities and that now she was being turned down due to her age. Despite an incredible CV, younger girls were getting the jobs. However she persevered, and a few months later she joyfully announced that she had been offered a role in a business that had just let a younger, unreliable and unsuitable employee go. Ruth had walked in just at the right time, and now the office is thriving due to her capable input. Ruth's attitude and determination gave her the courage to persevere. We need a lot of that to prove our value in this fast-moving world.

We never really know what's going on in others' lives. We see an exterior display which can actually be quite different to inner emotions. Behind brave, confident and self-assured behaviour may be recent recovery from illness, job loss, or even loss of a family member.

Many actors, musicians, athletes, politicians and business people emanate a certain attitude that they are in control of their lives, but they too have been through tough times in the past – or may be experiencing them right now.

No matter what your circumstances are, attitude gives you a certain air of confidence and certainty, which draws people together. It creates a feeling of safety, security and success.

CHAPTER 5

Your Personal Style

It's trendy to be sixty now – and if you doubt that, just check out the enormous Instagram reaction to images of women with attitude who are in their sixties, doing interesting things, and looking fabulous.

Would you love to mix things up a little?

If you do want a change, creating a new personal style doesn't mean buying an expensive wardrobe of new clothes. If you have always stuck to one style, a few basic colours, the same hairstyle, or the same shade of lipstick, I encourage you to consider livening up your image, as I believe this will also liven up your life.

You will find that your new personal style will permeate your life in both subtle and more dramatic ways. A new hairstyle or a more colourful wardrobe will boost your confidence. You might choose to drink orange juice out of a wine glass, or tea in a beautiful bone china cup and saucer. You might ride a scooter wearing bright lipstick with hair flowing, or throw your leg over a bloke's bicycle wearing cycle pants.

I have always worn one long earring on one ear and two studs on the other. It's unusual, and people do say 'Oh yes I remember you; you wear odd earrings!' But it's who I am, and I do it because I lost so many single earrings, and friends now give me their one-offs as well. I now have loads of wonderful single earrings and change them constantly.

I've never been a hat person, feeling they are an unnecessary accessory, but now in my sixties I love the look of hats on mature women. They are so demure and stylish, and they add interest and attitude. Pinterest has wonderful images of some dramatic hats on stunning women, and I have tried many as I travel, and now love them. Not being a natural hat person I need to coax myself to wear them, just because they give me so much pleasure.

Women are becoming bolder and some choose to have a tattoo as a personal style statement. I suggest a henna or fake one is the way to trial the idea, as I will always remember how having a real one done on my ankle many years ago hurt like hell! If it's a fake, you can always change it. It's fun, makes you giggle and is quite ridiculous but why not?

Style is something
that each of us
already has.
All we need to
do is find it!

Many women in their sixties and beyond dress stylishly and look sensational: just look at Madonna, Ellen De Generes and Meryl Streep, for example. Closer to home we have fabulous women like Lee Lin Chin, Margaret Pomeranz, Maggie Beer, Jenny Kee, Maggie Tabberer, and so many more.

They are all known for their unique personal styles, and may inspire you to create a similar style.

Use social media sites like Pinterest and Instagram to seek out inspiration. Here are a some women who exude a confident and unique personal style – and there are so many more:

@funkingafter50

@susanrayne

*@_stillstylin_*

If you would like some hands-on assistance with your style update, you can pay a stylist or a colour consultant to advise you. Otherwise you could turn to a friend who dresses more adventurously than you, and try on her clothes or shop together – what fun!

Here is my advice to help you begin your transformation to trendy. Let's get started.

Step 1

Sit in front of a mirror and take a good look at yourself. Smile! What do you see? You are not looking for perfection. You are what you are, and you have to like what you see. Decide now to like that woman in the mirror – she deserves it. Smile again at the secrets you share with her. That's a good thing!

Your wrinkles tell your life's story, so accept them as part of you. We all have them, and I will never mess with mine, although I know many women turn to cosmetic surgery or injection fillers.

Have regular facials, use quality skincare and makeup, and wear sunscreen every day, because they do make a huge difference to your skin. It's the vitality in your face that matters, not the wrinkles. A healthy, happy face is beautiful regardless of age.

(I recommend you take a look at Sarah Jane Adams' Instagram account. What a great attitude – her wrinkles are her stripes: @mywrinklesaremystripes)

Step 2

If you have worn the same safe look for many years, your sixties is a time for creating a unique new look with style and flair. Look through some magazines and tear out a few fashion ideas you would like to try. The process can be subtle at first – add a designer scarf and some bold new earrings.

Opp shops and recycled clothing boutiques are a perfect starting place, and many are quite upmarket. Experiment until you feel brave and comfortable. Rather than shying away from change, embrace it and enjoy yourself.

Check out your wardrobe. Is it made up of all blacks and beiges? It may be time to make room for some new ideas. Throw out anything you've not worn for two years, or that doesn't fit. If that is a struggle, arrange a try-on session with a friend or stylist.

Remember, you are not too old to wear jeans! Every woman needs at least one pair as they are the perfect option in many situations. A sixty-year-old woman in a pair of well-fitting jeans with a crisp white shirt and soft scarf looks very chic. Shoes with a heel allow you to strut with confidence.

Step 3

Does your hair flatter you? Are the colour and cut right for your face? This is a perfect time to go natural or create a flattering silver look, which many younger women are now choosing as well. Feel free to be bold and experiment – and not follow the latest mass trends. A good hairdresser, the right colour, an edgy cut, and a beautiful conditioning treatment can turn your boring, drab hairstyle into gorgeous, healthy-looking hair that instantly gives you vitality and style – and lifts your spirits!

You can be
gorgeous at thirty,
charming at forty
and irresistible
for the rest
of your life.

—Coco Chanel

Step 4

Do you wear colourful, daring, lacy bras and knickers every day? I do! If we put these on in the morning, what a fabulous start to the day, don't you think – even if no-one else sees them. We can secretly smile about what we are wearing beneath our clothes during the day, creating endorphins which make us happy.

Have you dared to try a G-string? I did once and felt I should be arrested for an indecent act in public as I tried to extract the tiny strip of fabric from my bottom! They are dreadfully uncomfortable compared to our matronly 'Bridget Jones' knickers, but go on – they will make you laugh. You may feel that the whole world can see your cheeks moving, but the 70-year-old coming your way might be wearing one too!

Step 5

Share the goodness! Start complimenting others on their appearance. It's such a wonderful thing to do and people are lifted to another dimension by your kind comments. Be sincere of course. Don't you love it when someone compliments you?

Start with people you meet regularly – neighbours, fellow workers, family and friends, then extend to women you don't know so well. Don't be put off by those who ignore you or look at you strangely, as deep down they will appreciate your compliments. Your compliments feed the soul – yours and theirs.

*Style is knowing
who you are
what you want to say
and not giving a damn!*

—Unknown

Step 6

Go back to Chapter 3 and look at your Circle of Life, then ask yourself the following: What was I wearing during those decades? What were my favourite outfits? What 'look' did I choose at that stage of my life? Write down some fashion words on the lines below to remind you.

My twenties: ....

My thirties: ....

My forties: ....

My fifties: ....

Have you been making similar choices every decade? Did you have a certain look – or were you a bit wilder when you were younger? You now have an open slate to choose how you want to evolve in your sixties. What will it be?

Are you going to stay on the same page – or will you turn to a new one? Make your pledge here.

My sixties style will be: ....

Evolve with age. To say you want the same style at 25 as at 45 is a mistake.

—Stacy London

Step 7

Evaluate your personal style. This extends to your home, your furnishings, your leisure time, your mode of transport and the places you visit. In our sixties we can create value by investing time, and indulge in enhancing our personal space, and enjoying life. Even small, subtle changes can create happiness and add value to our life.

Take a look at your home: is it a reflection of you, whether or not you own it or rent it? What areas can you transform to reflect your style, and enhance? Look at interior design magazines. Maybe focus on a feature wall or picture window. Consider designing a corner for reading or exercising. Change your décor with artwork and accessories such as bright cushions and rugs – or replace old furniture with a few quirky pieces. Include colours that brighten your space and spirit.

How long have you had your current car? Are you ready for a new one? Can you afford to replace it? Choosing a new car in a colour you love is thrilling. We spend so much time driving, so make it a pleasure by creating a personal space with magazines for traffic jams, hand cream, have iced tea or lemon water in your cooler, and make sure you have great music to listen to.

A bicycle or scooter is a freedom vehicle that gets you out and about, and in touch with your neighborhood. Imagine riding to your favourite café in the morning or evening, enjoying the fresh air. I love the retro-looking coloured bicycles with rattan baskets at the front, reminiscent of the ones we used to ride.

Step 8

Make the time to discover new things, and find out what you really enjoy. In urban areas we all have access to many free arts, sporting and community events and facilities. Check out what is around you.

If you've never spent much time in an art gallery or museum, now's the time. Visit one or more regularly and absorb the art on display. It can also be great fun going to gallery openings and watching people, especially arts buffs – and learning more about art of course. And there is usually free champagne and canapes.

Keep informed about new exhibitions. Make a note of musical events and arts festivals, and put the dates in your diary or to-do list. Don't miss the wonderful experience of outdoor performances in vineyards, jazz concerts, recitals and theatrical events. Immersing yourself in the arts world will not only increase your knowledge of various art forms and talented artists but will also increase your social connections and connect you with a varied group of personalities.

If you love reading, don't simply sit at home and read that book alone: take it out with you! Meet other book lovers by joining a book club. Read outdoors, in libraries, at the park, at the beach, by the river, or in a field under a tree. How wonderful – just add a rug and small picnic.

One of my personal passions is spending time in upmarket hotel foyers whenever I get the chance. I just love the style and atmosphere of elegant artistic interior design in an ambience of grandeur, comfort and exquisite taste, as well as quality artwork and beautiful floral arrangements. My chosen foyers are as valuable and impactful to me as it would be if I were invited to a palace, the home of a celebrity, or a private castle. I am transformed for a while! Yes it is an indulgence but it's one I can easily fulfil at home and overseas. If I choose to partake, the beverages and food served in these high-end foyers are expensive but they are created by talented chefs, chosen for their creativity and culinary skills. So I stay for as long as possible to justify the cost!

In my sixties, creative design, the art and flavours of fine food, and the delight of drinking from a cocktail glass are all passions in which I can indulge in many stunning hotel foyers. These special times are also an excuse to dress up, uplevel the mood of my environment, spend time with myself, view the world from a comfortable chair and enjoy good food and music.

I seek out and spend a lot of time in hotel foyers in every country I visit, meeting friends and family, reading magazines and newspapers, and even writing this book. It gives me so much pleasure – plus there are always interesting people coming and going to watch and wonder about.

We have access to such diversity today. Movies, shows and books may shock us, test our boundaries and force us to question our principles. We will either love or hate bizarre fashion styles. Art galleries and museums display weird and wonderful artwork and artifacts. Ladies in their sixties and seventies are choosing fashion that is wild and daring – and I say why not?

Our sixties are about truly recognising the person we have become, knowing what it takes now to make our heart sing, and living that courageously in our everyday world – with the audacity to go against the grain whenever we wish.

Great personal style is an extreme curiosity about yourself.

—Iris Apfel

CHAPTER 6

Staying Alive

For more than sixty-three years I have woken up each day and thanked my body for supporting me all the way! It is a magnificent thing, this body of mine. Yours is too. Let's not take this precious gift we are all blessed with for granted one more minute.

You know that we are the most fortunate lot of sixty-year-old women ever. Medical breakthroughs mean that we may no longer require chemo for early onset of breast cancer, and keyhole surgery has replaced major surgeries of the past. Imagine the future where perhaps one day we may walk through a frame (rather like the metal detector at the airports) which detects all illnesses and bodily malfunctions and adjusts them accordingly! That may become a reality for people coming after us.

Meanwhile, let's not rely on medical discoveries: let's take responsibility and follow preventative health measures to ensure all parts of the body are working to their full capacity.

Time for an honest conversation. How well are you taking care of yourself? Do you:

- Breathe deeply?
- Drink enough water?
- Eat healthy food?
- Move your body?
- Meditate?
- Sleep well?
- Relax and pamper yourself?

Let's take a closer look at each of these essentials.

Breathe: It's our lifeline, and this basic, simple and enjoyable routine will do wonders.

First thing in the morning, either in bed or in a beautiful spot, take ten deep breaths to wake up your system. It feels wonderful. Slowly and deliberately breathe in deeply and then release it. This simple exercise revitalises the body and you are ready to go. If you do this a few times a day, that's an extra bonus for your system.

Drink water: Two litres daily are a necessity for your body to function well; and dehydration can have a visible impact on your appearance.

A litre of water first thing in the morning kick-starts your bodily functions. Water replenishes the body as it does to a wilted plant, particularly as we age. It gives an instant rejuvenation that bounces the body to life, giving us clarity and a sense of wellness to move into our day.

Drinking water is like washing out your insides. The water will cleanse the system, fill you up, decrease your caloric load and improve the function of all your tissues.

—Kevin R Stone

Eat healthily: Eat quality food to keep your major organs in good working order for many years to come.

We are besieged in the media with the latest food trends and discoveries, which literally change every week! Chocolate is bad for you one day … but wait … it contains anti-oxidants which are good for you. Too many eggs or not enough? How many cups of coffee are safe? And as for wine – there are even recent warnings about quaffing even one much anticipated glass of wine a day! Then we have the ongoing debate about organic versus non organic.

Feeding our bodies well is of ultimate importance. My best advice is to completely ignore all supermarket advertising and focus on the simple things that keep our bodies well. That, simply, is called *clean food*.

Think about it! The things that upset our insides, make us tired, mess with our skin, and affect our moods, are the extras, additives, pre-made mixes and over-cooking of prepared food. Hotel buffets, boarding school meals, hospital canteens or corporate function dishes are usually swimming in a heavy sauce, laden with additives.

The alternative choice is to consume what's called a healthy artisan of cooking. Today chefs are taking us back hundreds of years to simple, clean food and it's delicious! Let me explain.

Take tea for example – what is it exactly? Leaves, of course. The big tea companies process many thousands of tea bags, requiring machinery, preservatives and transportation. Instead, pick some herbal leaves from your garden, such as mint, or steep a piece of lemon, lemongrass or lemon myrtle in hot water. Or buy locally: the fresh and natural teas sold in markets are delicious.

I love a simple lunch of pepper trout, fresh steamed asparagus, half an avocado, and a couple of boiled potatoes with butter, salt and pepper. Simple, tasty clean food, not smothered with white or cheese sauce made from white flour, milk and hard cheese.

To eat cheese or not – that is another question! I prefer to purchase locally and from small businesses as the cheeses are fresh, not overly processed, and are made with love. I make the same choice with bread as I never buy a loaf in a plastic bag from a supermarket. Bought fresh from a local bakery, the quality and taste are incomparable. The delicious aroma alone stirs up the digestive juices and contributes to what healthy food is all about – savouring, tasting and enjoying.

The benefits of clean food are enormous and we should accept nothing less. It feeds our cells and blood stream with nutrients rather than toxins that our livers struggle to eliminate. At sixty, toxins force our bodily functions to work on overload and slowly but surely break down. Our liver, intestines, immune systems and sleep patterns suffer. Food has evolved so much in our lifetime, and we have travelled and tasted wonderful cuisines from all over the world. Surely we do not want fast food any longer!

I met Joan, nearly 65, overweight, short in stature, her hair and skin dull. She attended my Meetup group and always made us laugh. She then missed a few meetings, and turned up again, some weeks later. I gasped on seeing the glint in her eye, her big smile and the wonderful glow about her. She also had a new hairstyle and colourful outfit. When I complimented her she said: 'I decided to live and eat clean, Chris, that's all. I'm eating clean food and it's doing wonders to my skin and my health. I've even lost weight.' Joan was on a mission to change from being sluggish and lacking purpose to feeling fantastic throughout her sixties.

Keep moving: When your body is unchallenged it becomes undisciplined. Without movement your joints, muscles and flesh deteriorate.

Advances in technology mean that our lifestyles have changed. We're spending a lot more time sitting down – at home, at work and travelling. The benefits of movement such as stretching, walking and swimming can be profound. For starters, you'll burn more calories, assist weight loss and increase energy. Even better, the muscle activity needed for standing and other movement seems to trigger important processes related to the breakdown of fats and sugars within the body. When you sit, these processes stall and your health risks increase. When you're standing or actively moving, you kick the processes back into action.

Food is the most abused anxiety drug. Exercise is the most under-utilized anti-depressant.

—Unknown

Today, health and wellness are part of a massive industry. Consider what type of exercise you will enjoy. Don't kid yourself by saying you will go to the gym each day, if you don't like gyms. So what are your alternatives – and what fits into your day to add value to your life? There are many good choices but my favourite that has worked for me for decades? It is walking!

Walking is the most natural exercise for the human body, and it's free! When you walk you are free of cost, and free to decide where to go, for how long, what to wear, how to walk, what time of day or night, and whether to walk with someone or alone.

Firstly, decide how long you will walk – fifteen minutes, half an hour, or one hour? Before you walk, remember to stretch. Divide your time in two, walk out in the first half, then return to keep track of time and build confidence.

Walk yourself out
of a bad mood.
Studies show that even a
ten minute walk
immediately boosts
brain chemistry
to increase happiness.

—Karen Salmansohn

While walking, your entertainment options include:

1. No music or added sounds, just those around you. Create your walk of 'mindfulness', breathing out toxins and filling your body with oxygen. Take deep breaths and allow your mind and body to clear thoughts of the past, the future and today. Appreciate the environment and the weather, and notice what is around you.

2. Your playlist. Create a playlist of your favourite songs. Move to the music and swing your arms. You might find yourself smiling and moving with a hint of a dance! Take longer strides and check if any part of the body is hurting or stiff? Maybe stop and do some stretches – you can do anything to good music!

3. Follow a fellow walker! Be on the lookout for a walker on a mission. Always follow someone better than you, because whatever they are doing will benefit you. I've often done this because it's inspiring to watch someone else – and it makes for great motivation.

4. Time to Learn. Download interesting apps onto your iPhone to keep you stimulated and focused. Listen to Ted Talks, international news, 'how to' talks, general knowledge … or you could even learn a language while you walk. Now that adds value to value! Make sure that you have good earphones: though I generally

use only one in my ear so I can hear traffic and people.

5. Focus on Weights. Once you have found your groove you could add weights as you walk. They are very effective for strengthening upper bodies at our age. Swing your arms or lift them to keep arm muscles toned. Optional ankle weights keep calf and leg muscles strong also.

6. Group Walking. Walking with other people is a good motivator. There are many casual Meetup walking groups where walking becomes a personal fitness agenda and a social connection. Walking is so much fun – enjoy!

Meditate: Meditation focuses and concentrates your mind, and helps maintain optimum functioning as you age.

It simply offers a time to pause, to focus the mind on calm and stillness – nothing more, nothing less. It's like driving long distance then simply pulling over, turning off the engine and taking a break. We know that our cortex shrinks as we get older and we find it harder to figure things out and remember things, however studies have shown that fifty-year-old meditators have the same amount of grey in the prefrontal cortex matter as twenty-five-year-olds.

Many Meetup groups focus on meditation, yoga and breathing classes. Fitness centres also hold meditation classes. There are numerous apps available that alert you that it's time to take time out. My smart watch also has a calming app and every so often it reminds me to take a break. I'm always surprised how my heart is racing, or my thinking is out of control when I am reminded to rest, and I feel an instant calm and a slower pulse when I use this app.

Sleep: Similar to re-booting your computer, a good sleep regenerates the body system.

Sleep is a long pause, a switch-off time to re-boot and revive all working parts of the mind and body. We know that some young people today find it hard to switch off and sleep due to overuse of technology. At our age, hopefully we know how to wind down in the evening, by preparing ourselves with a hot bath or shower, a warm drink and a quiet environment. We must honour the ritual and enjoy the experience. I find that I need less sleep as I get older but more importantly I sleep in shifts.

How many of us actually get six or seven hours uninterrupted sleep at sixty-plus? Toilet visits are usually a necessity and getting back into a deep sleep is never guaranteed.

Because of the responsibility I have at my work, I make sure I have a 'power nap' at 2pm each day, for ten to twenty minutes, to give me an energy boost for the rest of the day and evening.

*Meditation is a vital way
to purify and quiet
the mind,
thus rejuvenating the body.*

—Deepak Chopra

Pamper yourself: Nothing beats pampering and massage to relax the system and put a smile on your face.

Massage is a manual therapy that manipulates muscles and tissues, and also affects the nervous system. It provides relief from stress, muscle tension, pain and stiffness; and it relieves joint aches and pain and headaches. Lasting anywhere from sixty to ninety minutes, a massage increases circulation, helps recovery before and after joint surgery … and the list goes on. Using a variety of strokes and different techniques, a good therapist delivers a significant amount of relief in a few treatments. Massage therapy is typically performed with oil or lotion, but can be done without, as for a sports massage. Always check with your doctor first to ensure a massage will not cause problems for you, as there are some precautions in some cases.

Health retreats claim that 'massages are a necessary indulgence' – don't you love that! In our sixties we need every trick in the book to live life to its fullest, and we should choose what is best for us. We have worked hard at life and pushed our bodies to extremes. We have endured stress, disappointment, deadlines, and responsibility for others during long days and nights – all taking a toll on our bodies.

Sleep is the
Golden Chain
that binds
health and our bodies
together.

—Thomas Dekker

Some women claim they don't have the time for a massage, or can't find anyone to look after the family. Now it's time to claim your time!

I suggest an Aromatherapy or Swedish massage for total relaxation and enjoyment. Your whole body will completely relax and shut down into a blissful state of euphoria. The only thing you must ensure is that you don't fall asleep – because you don't want to miss it!

****

Two other enjoyable forms of exercise I can highly recommend are deep water running and dance.

Deep Water Running: Working out in water is effective, painless and enjoyable. At sixty, our bodies prefer low impact movements, making exercising in water the perfect choice. Join a class to begin with, and use a swim belt to get going and learn the movements. Start with aqua jogging for half an hour, making bicycle movements with your legs in the water. Vary your leg movements, wider or smaller and faster. Pause with legs straight and make little flutters with your feet, moving up and down. Next, twist your hips from side to side with arms out stretched and legs straight. Cup your hands and moving your arms forward and back to strengthen your arms and shoulders. This in itself is a great cardiac exercise and your half hour will be up before you know it.

Dance: Every girl was born to dance. As children it was natural; at sixty we still have the joy in us! Dancing is

You can't by happiness
but you can buy
a massage,
and that's
kind of the same thing!

—Anonymous

more than exercise and movement; it is mood, rhythm, style, breathing, music – and letting go of stress in our tense and stiff bodies.

Choose any style you like - salsa, country, hip hop, Nia, ballroom or line dancing, to name a few. Let yourself go and flow with the music. The freedom of natural movement to music that lights you up will make you feel happy, and will free your spirit to sing again.

> *During a Meetup event with me, Audrey, aged 64, announced that she had taken up ballet dancing and recently bought a pair of pointe ballet shoes. Although she was slightly built, we all gasped at the thought of her standing right up on her tippy toes! She shared that she had learned ballet when very young, and life had gotten in the way and not allowed her to follow her passion. Recently she had found a ballet class for mature women who wanted to dance at their own pace. She said the music was so soothing, and the personal space practicing at the bar brought back memories of her childhood. She loved*

these classes and being dressed in her gracious ballet dress and shoes put a smile on her face!

Some cities hold 'Dancing in the Dark' or 'No Lights no Lycra' classes where people move to wonderful music virtually in the dark, seeing only the silhouettes of others. I have tried this and honestly it's fun: such freedom to move and be yourself. Dance is a tonic for the soul, so give it a go!

****

Your quality of your life depends on how you honour and respect your body today. Scientists and researchers are responsible for ongoing discoveries and deeper understandings of the capabilities of our brain, heart, gut and lungs, and results prove that age alone is not the reason their functional abilities slow down.

Use your body well; get to know how amazing it really is; take care of it like it is a treasure – because it really is – and you will achieve amazing results.

CHAPTER 7

The Quality of Time

How true the saying: 'Time flies!' Time is such a precious and valuable commodity which we particularly need to acknowledge at this stage of our lives. We need to focus on how we spend our time otherwise we will regret seeing it slip away. I believe that the quality of the moment has nothing to do with the amount of time. I'm now 63 years old and actively preparing for my 60s decade because I want them to be my best ever! We women today have never been in such good nick and we have a strong mind-set to make things work.

As George Harrison wrote, 'It's being here now that's important. There's no past and there's no future. Time is a very misleading thing. All there is ever, is the now. We can gain experience from the past, but we can't relive it; and we can hope for the future, but we don't know if there is one.'

Speaking about time, we usually refer to it as a quantitative measure in terms of considering how much time do I have left? In the past people were more concerned with the quality of time and almost ignored the quantity. The Biblical 'three score year and ten' meant as recently as last century that people were lucky to live beyond their seventies. Today we are living much longer and the United Nations projections are that there will be 3.7 million centenarians across the globe in 2050!

We women in the Western world have never been in such good shape as we are today, and we know how to make things happen. I'm now sixty-three years old and actively living my 60s decade the best way I can because I want it to be my best ever!

You define what
Is important to
You by what you
Dedicate your time to.

—Unknown

I suggest that you keep your Circle of Life handy (you did this in chapter 3) and refer to the activities you chose to focus on, to remind you of your values and what is important to you. Do you need to connect with someone you haven't seen for a while? Do you need a sea change, or a move to a place that intrigues you or has happy memories? Is there a sport or interest you have never tried, and should?

More importantly, your quality of time extends to who you spend your time with. Be careful you don't waste your precious time on people who do not enrich you. I am single and over the past few years I have dated quite a few men. To begin with, I accepted most requests and sometimes sat for endless hours listening to men speak about themselves, talk about their past, moan about their divorces, and whinge about how much money they still had to give to their exes! Their way of impressing me I guess!

I then got a little wiser, and began agreeing to meet for a drink. I now accept a glass of wine and coolly assess whether I am enhancing the quality of my time. Either I sit and listen, then choose to have dinner – or I cut him short and say: 'Thank you so much for the drink, but I'm going to go home now!'

I have decided my choices are to stay and listen and engage, or retreat to my bedroom haven, dive into bed with my laptop, my book, my phone (to laugh with my kids), skype with a girlfriend – and have another glass of wine!

Dear Men:
You might think she wants your car
Your money, house and
expensive gifts
But the right woman
wants your time
Your smile, your
honesty, your caring
And above all
You choosing to put her as
a priority in your life.

—Unknown

Just because I am single, please don't think that I don't believe that a wonderful marriage or relationship is the ultimate, because I definitely do. What a gift if you have one, because it involves a lot of effort, mutual understanding and self-awareness. However, if you are on your own or in a relationship that is less than perfect, please consider your own quality of time. Only you can assess whether it is enough, and if not, make any changes you want, as many women around the world are choosing to do.

I lived in Sri Lanka for three years, setting up a retail business established by two women friends. To promote the business I attended many networking events, a favourite being the Working Women's Networking in Colombo, attended by determined, vivacious working women who were so interesting to meet. Sri Lankan women are proud of their traditional dress and are always beautifully presented in elegant saris of many colours. They arrive at business functions looking so feminine and yet a force to reckon with!

Although the divorce rate in Sri Lanka is considerably lower than in European countries, male influences are still very strong, although this is changing as educated women want to take more control. More mature women, realising that some traditional values are no longer relevant, want to leave their marriages to improve their quality of life. These women have had the huge responsibility of the home, the children and the family business, with little opportunity for self-expression or the chance to develop their own skills and talents. They now want to connect with like-minded women and, most of all, they want freedom from household duties and family responsibilities.

****

Each morning I carry out rituals which set the scene for the rest of my day, and they are essential to my quality of time (please refer to Chapter 6). Firstly, I take deep breaths, drink a litre of water and do my stretches. Next, onto my to-do list, which can hold anything from writing an email to spending time in the library, visiting a friend or watching a movie, to researching the brain, or new findings in psychology. I like to keep myself accountable and alert in mind and body.

Travelling Trish lives up to her nickname. In her mid-sixties she has a 'just do it' attitude. Stories on her Facebook page reflect her adventurous spirit, seizing every opportunity to travel from her base in Australia to the US where she house sits, meets up with travelling companions, experiences many different cultures and activities. Her travels take her to places such as Iceland, the Mid-West, Cuba, New Zealand and a cruise to Vanuatu. Then she returns to our Meetup groups with wonderful stories about her adventures,

which are an inspiration for the rest of us

Many women in their sixties are working women with business responsibilities and deadlines – the faster the better – leaving us dizzy and exhausted from fulfilling other people's expectations. We have mobiles, Internet, iPads and home delivery dinner services. Fast food is the ultimate for eating quickly but disastrous for our quality of time. Do all these services improve our lives, or are we missing the point? What is your quality of time?

My friend Lilly, director of an educational institution in Sri Lanka, was really run down due to illness, and was simply working too hard. Over lunch one day I listened to her telling herself to take time out and change her work routine. I realised that she was compromising her quality of time as her poor time management was damaging her health, and impacting her students and staff.

It's interesting that we don't always follow the principle of looking after ourselves first so that we are better able to support others. Putting ourselves first means slowing down, looking at the bigger picture and valuing our own health and well-being so that we can better cope with everything in our lives. When we met up again a few months later, Lilly looked incredibly well, although I learned it had taken being rushed to hospital with a breakdown to make her realise that time and health wait for no-one!

Health and well-being retreats are increasingly popular now as people realise the importance of preventative or curative self-care in an increasingly stressful world. At a health retreat you might learn more about clean food, essential movement, and essential stillness.

It is quite ironic, isn't it, that we work so hard to make money to survive, then spend it treating our run-down selves. If you have a high-level or demanding job, make sure that your mind and body can cope with the stress, anxiety and emotion which come with the package.

Typically, as women, we give to others first so be careful to replenish and feed your soul.

Meet Lucy, aged 61, a mother of four, grandmother of two and a busy real estate agent. Over coffee, Lucy excitedly exclaimed: 'I've just done it!' After ten years of being unable to travel due to family and job commitments, she had just booked a trip to South America to walk the Inca Trail – a lifelong dream. Her energy field had changed and she was now off on an adventure, talking about what to take, the places and people she could visit. In what seemed like a blink, she was back again, and over coffee we talked about her adventure and how she must book something else soon! She had acknowledged that quality of time was a precious gift to herself.

Time is free,
But it is priceless.
You can't own it,
But you can use it.
You can't keep it,
But you can spend it,
Once you've lost it
You can never get it back

—Unknown

Having been around for sixty-plus years, we all have so many memories and experiences to share. Use your precious quality of time productively. Why not research and write family memoirs for future generations? Or try your hand at poetry or creative writing? With the accessibility of courses on the Internet, you have the freedom to give so many things a go, an exciting prospect at any age.

At my 'Power of Women in our Sixties' Meetup groups I am inspired by women who have chipped away at learning something new. Raising children, managing family life and holding down a job have made us capable women, and we now deserve every opportunity to develop ourselves. At these events I watch the reaction of some women who have held back (for many valid reasons) as other women tell how they have recreated their lives. Their inspiration often leads to enlightenment and change for others.

When working in Bali I met two vivacious Australian women in a Balinese cooking class attended by about fifteen women from all over the world. Our host asked us to introduce ourselves, and the last two women were unforgettable. The first said that she had divorced her husband of 25 years recently, to move to Bali and start a hairdressing business. There wasn't a problem with the marriage, she said, she simply wanted to move on and have an adventure while she could. Her grown-up family understood and were very supportive, even excited about the prospect. The second lady then stood up and introduced herself. She too was getting a divorce, but her husband didn't know at this stage! She planned to move to Bali to join her friend in starting up a hairdressing business and become involved in the culture and lifestyle. Explaining that she still loved her partner, she simply didn't want to play the role of wife anymore, and wanted freedom at this stage of her life. Her husband was quite content watching sport on TV, happy with his group of friends and comfortable life.

These ladies left me with two things to think about – firstly, that ex-partners can remain friends. The world is full of compassionate, supportive husbands who may welcome the notion of a different and more productive relationship than before.

Secondly, many relationships stagnate and it is a bold move to open up a discussion about exploring alternatives that might make both partners happier. It could even prevent divorce and the inevitable financial and emotional trauma.

Can you imagine if the husbands of the women in the story were to say: 'I understand your need to do something different. By all means, go off to Bali and do your thing and I'll make regular visits and help if needed. In the meantime, I'll enjoy my mates and footy back home'. If this were to happen, everyone would benefit from increased quality of time.

Whether you are married or single, your choice is to either let life pass you by and one day wish you had lived it to the full; or to live the best life possible. You may have to compromise or change course, but with an open mindset the possibilities are endless.

Our sixties decade is ripe for excitement, yet the worry of lack of security, insufficient money and possible health issues – coupled with a 'too old' mindset may be deterring you from taking up opportunities for positive change.

If you plan to work towards something special each month, how satisfied you will be looking back on the year and reflecting on your achievements and adventures.

You know you have created valuable Quality of Time when you can look back and remember stories that start with: 'Oh my God, did I really do that?' Or: 'Do you remember the wild hippy party in full swing when your fiancé (who you hadn't invited because he was a bore) turned up?' Or … 'I can't believe we really put an ad in the paper and met all those guys!' … or 'I laughed so much because … '

Let's continue creating stories – because there is no reason to stop.

Here are some ideas to consider: some may make you gasp in horror, but you will consider doing others, I'm sure!

- Go on a road trip with friends
- Get a tattoo (fake is fine)
- Go skinny-dipping (safely)
- Test-drive a very expensive model of car
- Single ladies – ask someone out on a date
- Married or partnered ladies – show off your bright new bra and matching knickers
- Splurge on something extravagant (but don't blow your budget)
- Purchase something wild at the op shop
- Conquer one of your biggest fears
- Participate in the Mardi Gras or Oktoberfest
- Walk the Camino de Santiago
- Go skydiving
- Live abroad or housesit in another country
- Throw a large themed party that gets people talking
- Go glamping

- Forgive someone for hurting you
- Throw an upmarket dinner party for charity

With every decision, ask yourself this: Is this adding value or compromising my quality of time? Carpe Diem!

Don't under-estimate me.
I know more than I say,
think more than I speak
and notice more than you realize.

—Unknown

CHAPTER 8

Relationships

What a complex thing family is. We don't choose them – and each member is an individual, with so many energies, expectations, rules, dimensions, and complexities. The traditional concept of family held in our parent's generation has dramatically changed, and today's family is often a conglomerate of straight, gay, single, coupled, divorced, re-married parents, step-parents, children, half-siblings, grandparents, partners, ex-partners, step-grandparents of all ages, stages and mindsets.

A family can be a complex extended tribe with an assemblage of opinion, story, history and agenda. Now that's a force to be reckoned with! In our sixties, many of us have moved on from being the nucleus of the family. However, if you are still responsible for elderly parents, your own children, grandchildren or extended family, it's important to create a space for yourself so you are not overwhelmed by responsibility for others.

> *While out cycling recently I stopped at a surf club for a coffee. Waiting in the queue, I watched a couple with their adult autistic son in a wheelchair and my heart went out to them. The husband was so attentive, giving emotional and practical support while the wife was feeding their boy. I was wondering if they ever get any respite when two ladies stepped up and suggested they both go for a walk while they cared for their boy. The parents, like me, were overwhelmed with gratitude to have the chance for a short break. Such human kindness is a joy to see.*

I am twice divorced, with a son and a daughter, so my family is comparatively manageable. However, each of us make choices and deals with relationships as we see fit. My son's and daughter's relationship with their father is their affair, as it is with their stepfather, their grandparents, and other sister – and of course with me. They are adults now, formed by a lifetime of family experiences that allow them to choose and create their own relationships.

My daughter and her partner Chris have the most wonderful relationship. They have taken life head on steering their path where it takes them. Chris has two wonderful kids from a past relationship and I have now known them for over eight years. About five years ago little Jack came up to me and said, "How come you are Chris when Dad is called Chris?" to which I answered, "Well my name is Christine, but my friends call me Chris." He ran off to play and returned a while later to say," Well, we should call you Lady Chris!". I loved this because instead of taking it as just being the female version of Chris, I suddenly had a royal title. I was gob smacked and quickly answered, "I would like that!".

It's wonderful as when we are in a restaurant, the two kids run up to share something yelling, "Lady Chris, Lady Chris" and tell me their story. Those nearby look over to see who the important person is! Families are so diverse and if they are comfortable with theirs, at our age, we can fit in where it best suits. Kids are so open minded, so accepting and just love to be listened to. My relationship with these two wonderful kids is simply to be there, to be who they want me to be and to enhance their moments.

I am a house mother in a girls boarding school and just love my responsibility. I choose to be in the company of young people who all have trust and belief in everything. The extended family unit is diverse and one cannot accept there is a 'presumed' family unit.

Therefore, when a young person comes up and says, "We want to call you Lady Chris", it's an honour and its now up to me to fulfill that role. Grandma, Nana, and the many other titles for us ladies may not fit in this modern world – so let us leave the young ones to choose!

I recently spent time with my daughter and son in their worlds. Their relationships, outlook, goals, energies, expectations and views on life are so different from what mine were at their age. They readily give each other advice and get away with it, but now I keep quiet because I realise that I learned my own stuff through my life's lessons, as they now must. It's fascinating to watch their journey and the decisions they make along the way.

Perhaps it is time for a relationship change with your children? Many will be adults, either leading their own lives, testing the world in ways we do not always agree with, or, in your eyes, making mistakes in life. I say, let it go! Unless they are unwell or in dire need of your assistance (in which case they are lucky to have you) your children do not need you. Many people don't have parents at all and they cope really well. As someone once said, 'Children are a temporary responsibility. It comes to an end when they become adults and you start to live with them, not for them!'

It's not only children who grow
Parents do too
As much as we watch to see
What our children do
with their lives
They are watching us
To see what we do with ours!

—Joyce Maynard

In as much as children have to stop blaming their parents for 'everything', parents have to learn to regard them differently. This really is a great thing when we do, although it takes a concentrated effort as you have been so close for so long.

Both my kids, aged in their late teens, came to visit me in Queensland for a few days. Setting out for some grocery shopping, my daughter suggested she drive my car to the supermarket and my son held back the passenger seat to let me in the back while he moved into the front! I was a bit put out at the presumption of it all, but let it go. My daughter re-adjusted the driver's seat and the rear mirror whilst commenting on how uncomfortable the seat was. My son stretched out, turned all the dials on my already programmed radio, and put his hand out the window to adjust the outside mirror and, then tilted back his seat. They both suggested I buy a new car! I sat mesmerized in the back while my car was being transformed!

At the supermarket my kids chose the food and then at the check-out, I paid for it while they scooted back to the car with the full trolley! No such thing as browsing around the shops or having a coffee somewhere. Granted, I didn't have to do anything (except pay) or lift anything, I didn't drive or need to look for parking or make decisions and the whole trip was effortless. I liked some of their choices of food but not others in my kitchen. I was given a glass of wine and sat on a stool watching my son and daughter putting together a meal. They chopped and prepared, cooked and set the table. I didn't comment or contribute, just enjoyed. They poked fun at each other, showed off their cooking skills and gave each other the odd hug. It was so much fun; we laughed, remembered occasions, talked about family and friends and I found myself smiling and laughing and enjoying every minute. We ate a wonderful meal and they cleaned up, washed the dishes and left the apartment spotless.

However, the whole experience could have been very different. I could have insisted in driving MY car, told them not to touch anything, given them advice on what food to choose, insisted on a budget etc etc. But when I sat in the back of the car I decided to let it go. As for me it was just a thrill to have them around for a few days. The simplicities of my life and routine would go back to normal very soon.

Since that supermarket trip, my outings with my son and daughter are more precious. Now they are buying me flowers, treating me to lunch, working out recipes and cooking together. They take over the kitchen while I head to the bar stool to sip wine and listen to them chatting and I love it. We all live in different countries and yet we are as close as ever, respecting each other and yet supporting each other without being stifling.

Families today are more diverse than ever. Many live close by and others live overseas, visiting occasionally. Children who have attended boarding school like me, may either be so independent that they live separate lives or crave being part of the family after many years apart. Family traditions such as being with family at Christmas, standing when elderly people arrive and opening and closing the doors may be forgotten or respectfully preserved. Such courtesies may not be considered relevant due to gender equality or modern beliefs but personally I am delighted when a younger person steps forward to open a door, offers their seat or helps me with heavy luggage.

What is your relationship with your adult children? Go up and sit on your cloud and look down. Figure out what qualities you have that they will value enough to consider you as a best friend. Changing your expectations, attitude and intentions will result in a more valuable relationship in the future. Consider the following:

a) If you have a wonderful relationship which is accepted by both parties (you and your son/daughter) then leave it as it is, why disturb something that is good?

b) If you have a difficult relationship with your son or daughter, then **you** have to change, as they never will. It will be your effort and yours only, and you may find that you are at fault. It may take a while to develop this new attitude but it will be worth it.

When I attended Tony Robbins' five-day course *Date with Destiny*, he stressed that only you can change a relationship by doing everything within your power to give that other person what they want to receive. Not what you think they want, but what they want.

It is not what
you do for your
children, but
what you have taught
them to do
for themselves
that will make
them successful
human beings.

—Anne Landers

Letting go of a needy relationship is a hard one, especially if you are the needy person. It takes work, as it takes you out of your comfort zone, but it also opens you to other possibilities.

What if your son and daughter considered you as a friend, a mentor, and of value in their life? What if they invited you to meet their friends and included you in social gatherings? Or if they called more often and you listened rather than complained?

A mother's job
Is to teach her
Children not to
Need her anymore.
The hardest part
Of that job is accepting success.

—Unknown

If your children are mentally or physically handicapped, or face another issues, they are so fortunate to have your love and support. I hope you too have the best support possible. If not, find some or reach out to others in the same situation. Perhaps create a Meetup group for mothers or parents in similar circumstances in your area. If you just reach out, you will be amazed how people rally around. We women in our sixties are brilliant at supporting each other, but we often need to know our support is welcomed, otherwise we stay away out of respect for privacy.

When grandchildren arrive we are once again swept up with caring and loving the next generation, and hoping to be closely involved. At this time, once again, we need to pause, be strong and contain our judgement and opinions – but always be there with advice if needed. After all, we have been through the challenges and joys of babies and bringing up children. Things will work out well in the end; they usually do.

Friendships

A good friend is priceless. They allow you to be yourself and also allow you to consider them as special. Friends are everything as special people can enrich our lives. You can be yourself with friends, without judgement, and they understand you.

Friendship, like time, is about quality rather than quantity. If you have just a few close relationships, perhaps that's all you can cope with in your busy schedule. Perhaps you don't want or need a lot of emotional connections, and possible ups and downs.

I have some very special friends, women who allow me to be myself. Some are girlfriends I have known since boarding school, yet our separate journeys have added value when we re-connect and get to know each other again. Others are from my twenties, and our separate relationships and adventures since then would fill up a book itself! Then I have girlfriends who have come and gone in my life, and this makes meeting up when we can so special.

I was once told, 'Friends come in and out of your life all the time and it's important to let them go and embrace them back.' Sadly some friendships have lead to hurt, and it's only now that I can look back and accept that these are some of life's lessons.

At one of our Meetup group sessions, Ruth confided that she had accepted a couple of invitations to join us then had cold feet, so cancelled. She admitted that she was used to doing everything with her partner, and after he died a few years ago she felt self-conscious and

There comes a time in your life,
when you walk away from
all the drama and people
who create it.
You surround yourself with
people who make you laugh.
Forget the bad and
focus on the good:
Love the people who treat you right
and pray for the ones who don't.
Life is too short to be
anything but happy.
Falling down is a part of life,
getting back up is living.

—Jose N. Harris

daunted by the prospect of joining any new social group. She shared with me that it was the wording on the Meetup invitation that got her over the line: 'If it's your first time just do it. Come join us and you won't look back!' She finally plucked up the courage, came along, and soon she was happily chatting with others, then eventually shared her story. I laughed at the end of the session when she whispered to me that she had taken a mild sedative before the Meetup to settle her nerves, just in case!

It can sometimes take up to five or ten years to make a new 'best friend' so you had better start now. The Meetup group I've created has opened up new friendships for me, as I have met some exceptional women, all at my stage of life, each with a different journey – yet all with the same intentions, fears and hopes for the future. We are in it together.

Turning acquaintances into friends can be exciting or daunting, and we must accept that we won't love everyone – and everyone won't love us! You can be assured of one thing: everyone needs company at some time, so everyone is on the lookout for acquaintances.

You may find them in the local supermarket, at the doctor, dentist, library, hotel, school, church – anywhere, in fact. Some may become friends, some may not. That's fine.

Time is the currency of relationships. If you want to invest into your relationships, start by investing your time.

—Dave Willis.org

Let me tell you more about my adventures with Meetup, an online connection platform set up to bring people with common interests together in real life. It is now in 182 countries, and at the time of writing this book, there are 32.30 million members, 288,726 Meetup groups, and each month there are 614,764 Meetup events happening around the world.

How does it work? You set up an interest group within the platform (www.meetup.com), and with the help of the website team, your group is advertised to others in your area. Interested people join the group, and some will attend live events you organise. There is an incredible array of interest groups in Meetup, from arts to science and tech, and everything in between. I suggest you go online and search for what is happening in your area – you will be happily surprised.

I was turning sixty in the February of 2015 and promised myself that before the end of January that year I would create a new Meetup group called 'The Power of 60 Year Old Women'. I figured that if no-one thought as I did – that the power of amazing and interesting sixty-year-old women was worth meeting and sharing – then I could close it down and run away! I put something together and the group went live on the website.

Each day I logged in and checked numbers, and slowly but surely the interest grew. A few women signed up at first and then I advertised the get-togethers – a couple a month in different areas on the Gold Coast in Australia, at different times, mornings and evenings.

To Date, three years later, I have 520 members, have had 140 Meetup events, and I have met the most vivacious, interesting and authentic group of women in their sixties. It's been a real pleasure, and we continue to meet twice monthly.

Surround yourself with people who make you hungry for life. Touch your heart and nourish your soul.

—Unknown

CHAPTER 9

Loneliness

Lonely is not always alone.

A child can feel lonely when they are facing a challenge even though they may be within a family unit. A teenager can face loneliness when they are learning about their world – and that can be daunting. A young mother can feel alone when their husband or partner does not understand the reality of coping with a new baby. A man can feel alone when work challenges keep him from his family.

Oprah's magazine, *O*, has even established a project called 'Just Say Hello' to combat the growing epidemic of loneliness, and encourages people to connect face-to-face with neighbours, school mates and interest groups.

Electronic communication has impacted real world relationships for everyone, not just young people. In fact, the largest growth in users of Facebook in 2018 was with the 55- to 65-year-old-plus demographic.

Feeling unsure and lost is part of your path. Don't avoid it. See what those feelings are showing you and use it. Take a breath. You'll be okay. Even if you don't feel okay all of the time.

Loneliness at sixty-plus can be caused by many things. Maybe you have recently lost a partner due to death or divorce; maybe your parents have passed away, leaving a big gap in your life. Perhaps your children have moved away or your life has changed with retirement or redundancy; or you have moved somewhere unfamiliar and feel uncertain in your new surroundings. Perhaps you are lonely, yet not alone?

I truly believe that we can tackle loneliness head on in our sixties because most women seem to naturally love connecting and being together. We love to do things and work as a team to accomplish something satisfying. We are natural givers and have been for most of our lives – giving to family, work, friends and to those in need.

Located in one of the most beautiful areas in Australia, my Power of Sixty Year Old Women Meetup group regularly welcomes newcomers who have made the move here. One such lady was Dawn, who shared that after her husband died a few years ago she felt determined to remain in their house and continue life surrounded by friends and family. After a while she realised that she wasn't happy and knew she had to do something different. The big move came and went and she rented for a while to check out where she wanted to call home. At one of our Meetup events she met Pauline, who was also looking for a new place to live. They became friends and in due course decided to rent together to see if they were compatible before possibly buying. Dawn shared that the whole process had been so interesting and such fun that they were now about to sign a contract to buy their dream house together. I was in awe of her courage but as she said, she is happy now and if all goes belly-up, they have agreed to sell and move on.

Of course being alone can be wonderful and many people are that way by choice. When alone, the brain is activated more acutely as you can think, act and behave exactly as you choose. It's important to realise that you actually do have a choice – either to be by yourself or make an effort to be with someone.

If you are constantly surrounded by people, with little escape from noise, busyness, action, expectation or involvement, then solitude is probably just what you need more of.

When solitude becomes loneliness and begins to drag you down and change your level of energy, it can become a problem and may lead to depression. Before that happens, you have to take action, and find what is right for you. If you are a quiet, reserved person, you probably don't want to open up readily to someone you are not familiar and comfortable with. You simply need to adjust the balance of your life by adding the right company.

After my Dad died, I asked my mum if she was lonely. She said, 'I don't feel lonely, but I do feel alone.' They had been together for 59 years and been best friends throughout, so when Mum found herself alone, it must have been tough. She was the first to say that many of her friends and some family members hadn't been given the gift of experiencing their eighties, and who knows how long anyone has in life? The rest of her life needed to have value. She had been given this time to experience being alone, to see what her mission would be and slowly learn new techniques to cope with this huge change. Today she plays the piano in church each week, drives locally, emails, texts and WhatsApps with her grandchildren, and enjoys the community close to her.

There are pros and cons in most situations. I will never experience losing a life-long partner in old age as I have been on my own for many years. From a position on my cloud, I can look at everyone's lives and consider myself quite fortunate. I had both my parents until their eighties; I have a son and daughter in their thirties; and two ex-husbands – potentially avoiding the drudgery of a dreadful relationship! Plus I have loads of meaningful and precious friends. Life is what it is!

There have been many times in my life when I have felt lonely, but now I choose the solution to suit me. Once I thought that a partner would be the solution, but after all this time I realise that having one might be stifling. I now know that a 'partner on tap' would be ideal!

How great it would be to have a pool of people to choose from, depending on the circumstance. Having lived on my own for many years, I seek different companions at different times, such as a lunch or an event with a girlfriend, my son, daughter, their partners, or my mum. When out with them, we often seem to be amongst the very few at the venue who are actually enjoying their time and looking completely at ease. On the other hand, the times I have spent meeting a new man, and working out if there was any compatibility were exhausting.

Don't think too much.
You'll create a problem
that wasn't even there
in the first place!

Be unafraid to evaluate what is important to you. Time is one of the most valuable things you have now – and to have total control of that again can be a gift.

To help make the most of your time, I suggest you gather ideas for activities and create a 'Loneliness Fix-It Booklet' on your laptop or iPad, or in a funky notebook. Or you could simply do some mapping on a large A3 piece of paper using a variety of colours. Better still, how about creating a colourful vision board called something like 'Living!', made up of colourful magazine pictures and words, all representing the things you would like to try.

If your loneliness goes much deeper than just a lack of company, don't hesitate to seek guidance. Speaking up is the most important step. Be brave enough to speak with your doctor, your friends, family or phone a help line. You will feel safer and less lonely in the company of someone who cares.

****

I'll never forget the time I went out for dinner with a friend and her partner, who brought along a blind date for me. He was not my type so I left alone and drove home, wondering why I wasn't meeting the right guy. It was only 10pm on a Saturday night so, determined not to go home so early, I drove to a music bar

Never allow
loneliness to
drive you
back into the
arms of
someone you
know you
don't belong with.

and parked outside. 'Oh yes,' I thought, 'I am going to do this! No-one in there will know me: I'll just walk in as if looking for someone then walk out again.'

I got out of my car and approached the entrance. A security guard nodded me in and I headed to the bar where a few people stood around. The piano was in full swing, with many people on the dance floor. I ordered a lemon lime soda and waited. My goodness, what was I going to do now? I would have to turn around and face the crowd and make a decision. So I paid for the drink, took a big breath and turned. The place was packed and I just stood there, thinking. Spotting two ladies at a nearby table chatting together, I boldly walked over and asked if I could join them. They eagerly welcomed me and couldn't believe that I had walked in on my own. They shared that it took them courage to come here too and that they felt a bit nervous.

We all stayed way past midnight, chatting and dancing with those who asked us, and to this day I remember it as one of my really fun nights. The atmosphere was lively and everyone around us became friendlier as the evening went on. This boosted my soul, my confidence and my level of happiness, and as I drove home with a smile on my face I felt wonderful.

That evening changed my outlook on life and gave me renewed confidence that I could connect with others instead of sitting at home by myself.

****

To move out of your comfort zone, set an intention to achieve something that will boost your confidence. The company of like-minded people will make you happy – you just need to find them.

I suggest you make a habit of writing daily to-do lists. First thing each morning, start to fill it in and organise it, then feel your energy change. I suggest you write things that make you happy and rank these things on a scale of high to low.

Happiness lightens our load and can change our facial expression, creating positive energy and enriched thinking.

Your list could include:

- Go for a walk
- Go for a walk in the rain
- Walk to the park and sit on a bench
- Take close-up photos of buildings, flowers and people
- Go to a museum or art gallery and join a tour to be with people
- Go to a flower shop and buy flowers in colours you love
- Buy an art board, paper and paints and paint the scene from your window
- Buy a pot of mint, basil or other herbs to smell and taste – your senses will love you for it
- Buy seeds of seedlings plant and nurture
- Say hello to someone – you may make their day
- Join yoga or an exercise class to change your energy level
- Join a swimming class – deep water running and water aerobics are wonderful
- Have a coffee in a bustling cafe – one with magazines
- Watch a funny DVD or go to a good movie and buy popcorn!
- Browse in a book shop for a book you love
- Go to the airport and have a coffee watching the dynamics of people coming and going
- Visit the library and read magazines

- Take a ferry trip to feel the movement of water
- Visit a clothes store, pick five items of clothing you would never normally choose and try them on
- Search on the Internet for 'What's on in my city'
- Join a gardening group, singing group, drawing/painting group
- Buy a $6 recorder and learn how to play it from the Internet (I did!)
- Sign up to a computer class – Apple run amazing classes at their big stores

You might also like to volunteer, as research has shown that people who perform altruistic acts of kindness report an increased sense of purpose and meaning in their lives. Driving, reading to, visiting, serve a breakfast, assist at the Red Cross or hospital?

An excellent way to combat the feeling of despair caused by loneliness is to actually help someone else feel less lonely. This does not mean you have to take on their problem; you simply lead them to company, involvement or support. You really are giving them a gift of companionship and strength in themselves to change their situation. Try acting on this in a spontaneous moment with a gesture or suggested activity to someone who may be lonely. It will benefit you both. There are always the generous of heart who reach out - such an admirable trait of character. Charities and support groups are full of men and women with that special gift of giving of themselves. Why not try?

A simple place to start – when out walking, sit on a bench and when someone joins you, ask something like:

- How is your day so far?
- What are your plans for this lovely day?
- Aren't we lucky to be living in such an awesome place?

If you feel confident enough, you could have a pack of motivational cards with you and ask them to choose one. You could also make your own cards (they can all be the same) and give them out to people you feel might need a lift. You might be the one thing that changes their life too – you never know.

I have volunteerd at a 'Need a Feed' centre near me, where I met fascinating people. We helpers arrived at 5.45am to prepare the centre for about 20 to 35 people, setting out tables and chairs, plates, cutlery and so on, and breakfast is all over by 7am.

Listening to the plight of others is an emotional experience and makes you appreciate your own life a little better. I have found that those who have little and need less are always the ones to assist others.

Let's change the perception of loneliness by inviting people into our circle who will give us joy and who we can share our blessings with as well.

CHAPTER 10

Dating is Outdated

Joining an online dating service for the first time at age forty-seven was the start of an interesting journey for me. Allow me to share some cautionary tales.

On my own and through a second divorce, I thought that the Internet was the place to meet fascinating and interesting men, so why not try it out! I soon learned that while online dating is a useful tool to potentially find a partner, it is NOT a solution to finding instant love or security! But if you are on your own and want some male company, it is helpful.

I signed up to a free dating service and found it very difficult deciding how much I would reveal about myself, who I might attract, and how I would feel if no-one contacted me! If you decide to try it, understand that it's a way of getting out there – dressing up, meeting and greeting, then deciding whether to treat any meeting as just a social encounter … or take it further, leaving your heart exposed to cope with any emotions that follow.

I finally put together a profile and waited …

A couple of days later I received a message from **Stephen** (not his real name). He was a physiotherapist living in Sydney, with two kids from his first marriage. We exchanged a few emails and then he suggested he fly up to where I live, to meet, spend a day, take me to dinner and fly back. Wow, what a step forward this would be! So I said okay and a couple of weeks later I met him at the airport and drove him to dinner!

It's an interesting scenario when you haven't met someone in the real world and have been guessing what type of person they are from a photo. Trust me - often they are not quite what you envisage. Stephen was in fact a lovely guy, good looking, but (and frequently there can be a 'but') he was much shorter than me. Everyone has their own 'thing' and mine is height – any date has to be taller than me. With blonde hair and a lovely smile, he was great to talk to, but he was shorter than me – much. Over dinner though, we talked with great ease. He was fairly forward with his affection, then became extremely affectionate, then

Online dating helps
me meet and breakup
with someone
without leaving
the house!

really over the top! By the time our dinner ended I was ready to race out of there; however, he paid the bill like a gentleman and walked me to the car. Next came the big question – where was he staying until his return flight the following morning? He implied that since we got on so well he might stay at my place. I insisted we stick to plan A – he was to book his own hotel room, and the fact that he had not done so made me think he had tried this before. I drove him to a hotel area and said goodnight.

He flew back the next day and his next email was a little short of a proposal! He thought that because we got on so well, I should consider moving down to Sydney and move in with him. I couldn't believe what I read – this fast-moving Stephen was obviously a step ahead of me and I wondered what move I had made to give him any inclination this could even be a possibility! There were several more polite emails, then Stephen and I moved on.

Michael and I met at a café. He was well-built, with a lovely smile, had been married for a long time, and was still getting over his wife's death from cancer. We chatted comfortably and he suggested taking me on an adventure: he asked whether I would meet at his place and leave the rest to him?

The following Saturday I jumped into his four-wheel drive and he told me about life on his ranch, his horses, his kids and how lonely his life was now. We stopped at a country hotel, had a beer by the river, and continued inland to another hotel which was hosting a fancy dress birthday party. Being the only ones not dressed up we were called 'The Visitors' and met some fun people. After a while Michael suggested we have something to eat and we sat down with a couple of burgers.

Then it all changed. He grabbed my hand quite roughly and demanded: 'Do you always chat to anyone and everyone when you are with someone?' I said that I didn't understand his question to which he replied: 'You are with me so stay close and I will choose who to chat with.' He held onto my hand tightly and led me to a secluded table where we watched everyone else having fun. He was solemn and I was a little nervous.

We left at 10.30pm. Noticing that my phone had no signal, I felt quite apprehensive in his vehicle and took deep breaths. He put on some sad, slow music (obviously very familiar to him) and began singing to it quite loudly. He told me all about his wife, how hard it was nursing her and watching her die. I was quite teary for him until he told me how he bought all her clothes, and that he decided on everything they did together. Heavy stuff!

After a couple of hours we arrived back at his place and he invited me in, but I kept walking to my car and politely but firmly said I was going home. He didn't stop me, but goodness was I glad to be away and safe from that very emotional situation.

Pierre approached me on RSVP and I first thought, mmm ... he looks nice. He lived down the road and suggested we meet for coffee at the café nearby. I arrived first and then he turned up, normal looking and seeming very calm and sure of himself. We chatted easily and got on really well. A lovely smile goes a long way and soon we found ourselves meeting for a walk and a coffee or lunch and so time moved on to when I was quite looking forward to seeing him.

He was fairly reserved and it made such a change not being with an egotistic male companion. I was relaxed and enjoyed his company. Then one day he unexpectedly turned our relaxed conversation into intensive questioning about my stance on life from a female point of view, pushing his belief that women should be seen and not heard. This really took me back; this man I thought was so wonderful clearly had so much emotional baggage. His conversation and questioning focused on children and how our roles as parents should be forceful and commanding. Wow, I was so confused and found I was being protective of my kids and my ideals. It was totally exhausting, so much so that I backed down in an attempt to evaluate the situation.

So our meetings became less frequent and I didn't encourage any commitments. I was confused as things had started off so positively and casually, but then his underlying personality came out and dominated. It was sad but I didn't have the energy or interest to even pursue the questioning. So Pierre and I fizzled out!

After dusting myself off again, surfing through the Internet and pages of available men, I came across a wonderful photo and thought, my god this man is beautiful! I scrutinized the black and white photo of **Antonio**, very Italian-looking, handsome with lovely eyes, wearing a crisp white shirt and with the most wonderful smile. This guy appeared comfortable with himself and from his appealing bio, I found out he lived only an hour north of me.

Ha, always grab an opportunity I say, and so I sent him a 'kiss'.

Now this was the first time I had made the first move and thought I was so brave. But hey, people get married from meeting on these sites and it has to begin with a move. Let's face it, he could decline and that would be the end of it. Well, the kiss had gone through and I started the waiting game with so many scenarios going through my mind. How many women had he dated, where did he live, why is he single, or is he, and what would I do next?

Antonio replied!

Sure he kept me waiting but after a couple of days connecting, Antonio (of course) suggested that we meet in my vicinity as he was passing through on business and named a pub on a corner quite near to my home. What luck! I was very excited and thought, hey maybe there is something to this online connecting after all. My imagination ran away with every possibility as I imagined the happiness that lay ahead.

I took ages deciding what to wear, not too formal and yet not too casual but to show that I make an effort.

Men like well-dressed women, especially Italians who normally dress well. I settled for smart jeans with a casual yet flattering top, not so high heels in case he was the same height (I'm fairly tall) and off I went, excited, nervous and terrified all wrapped up together.

Parking the car I thought that at 5pm the pub wouldn't be too crowded. It's the most petrifying thing to walk into the unknown, feeling that the whole world is looking at you, knowing what your plight is! But head up, shoulders back and a casual, confident stride. The pub was nearly empty and I surveyed the scene. I was certain that I would recognize him – European looking, a glint in his eyes, amazing smile, self-assured and over six-foot tall. Almost immediately I felt a tap on my shoulder. I turned … and looked down to see a puny male wearing a scruffy singlet looking up at me with his hand on my shoulder.

'Hello Chris, I'm Antonio!' he drawled in a broad Australian accent.

I tried not to gasp but my disappointment must have been obvious.

'You aren't Antonio!' I exclaimed to this young, scrawny guy with a dreadful sleazy smirk on his face.

'Well seeing you're here, can I buy you a drink?' he asked.

My whole body seized up and I had to think very quickly. 'Yes, I'll have a red wine.' He headed to the bar.

This wretch had faked a photo on the site, lied about his height (and no doubt everything else) which infuriated me. Going for a drink gave me time to plan. When he returned I was ready. I accepted the glass of wine, threw it down in a couple of gulps, stood up and said: 'Don't you dare do this to anyone else on RSVP! You are a fraud and I won't hesitate to tell women if I see you on the site again.' I quickly left.

I was humiliated and knew I could do nothing about it except go home and be miserable. But driving back, I started to laugh at myself and realise how intense this dating game was. I was only seeking one compatible man; how hard could that be?

Then there was **Steve** … but not on the Internet!

I drove my BMW into the underground garage of my apartment block and couldn't help but notice him stretch into the back of his car. Swerving into my space I turned off the ignition and grabbed my bags from the back seat. Heading towards the lift I noticed a stunning young man watching me, his eyes focused totally on me, with a slight smirk. My legs nearly buckled and a tingling sensation ran through my body. His beautiful six-foot-two physique of broad shoulders, slim waist and rough curly blonde hair stunned me as if hit by bat.

'And who are you?' he asked. The cheek of him, asking me, a resident in my own block!

'More to the point, who are you?' I asked. 'As I live here …'

'So do I,' he answered. 'My name is Steve and I've just moved in with my mates on the second floor.'

'And I'm Chris, resident on the top floor, nice to meet you!'

He beamed a tantalising smile, 'I'm sure we will be seeing a lot of each other, have a great day'. With that he turned and bounded two steps at a time to his apartment.

I couldn't control the smile on my face and my whole body felt electrified. A rush of happiness permeated my entire soul and body. I felt awesome.

This is how one of my favourite relationships started! Steve was in his mid-thirties and I was forty-eight at the time. For more than three years we had one of the most laissez-faire relationships I've ever had – flirty, passionate and then intimate. He taught me so much about 'live in the now'; 'let it go'; 'take it or leave it'; 'laugh in the moment'; 'be generous of spirit' and more. We enjoyed three glorious years with no rules, no expectations, and living in the moment. My only ask of him was to tell me when he met someone else, and in due course he did. And then we moved on, no baggage, no hurt – just big smiles and the best memories!

****

I'm sharing this with you because, at our age, it's all about communicating and meeting new and interesting people. It's about stories, encounters and memories. If we get out there and create adventures for ourselves, we remain interesting. Online connections allow us to do this. We don't need to sit at home and believe we can't get out but we must also be sensible and realistic in knowing we have to be in charge. Whether we connect through on-line dating sites, Meet Up groups, our local community centres or inviting someone to join you – we need to just do it and connect with more people.

We need to be extremely cautious when going in to a live-in relationship at this stage as it can be a financial and emotional disaster. Allowing a man who has nothing or very little move in to our domain and rely on our assets and security can be financially catastrophic! Be warned! If you are contemplating this, it is essential to see a lawyer before allowing anyone to move in. Also, younger women who are financially independent due to hard work in training, qualifying and securing an excellent job need to be just as cautious

Jane was a young go-getter woman, late 50s with two daughters from a first marriage at various networking groups. Quite reserved at the start, I witnessed her growing confidence and lovely personality. She had set up her own business, paid off her home and was enjoying the company of her

little family. However, I then heard that she was in strife as she had fallen for a man who she had been dating for a few months and he had moved into her home. Not only that, his two children had moved in too and he expected her to simply embrace them under her roof!

Don't let your heart rule your head! If you have a naturally generous heart and spirit, have the courage to pull back and if need be, be tough enough to protect your hard-earned assets above all else.

The idea of having a partner to complement or support us is wonderful, but 'happily ever after' stories can change overnight once hard reality sets in. Many of us are financially secure after years of hard work and dedication, especially if we have also had children to support, and suffered financially through a split or divorce.

If you have had a series of failed relationships, or been attracted to partners who have not enhanced your world, do you really need another one?

I may seem to be advocating a sense of renewed freedom in relationships, but I am serious when I say to tread with caution when thinking about changing a love-in to a live-in.

And yes, I do believe dating is outdated! We can hold the reins and decide if we are going to approach someone to join us for dinner or a movie. Are we going to give someone the pleasure of our company – or politely refuse an invitation because we recognise the relationship potentially is not what we are hoping for?

Through the Meetup groups I have met many ladies who confidently dress up and go out with the intention of meeting a partner. I'm in awe of their confidence as they simply know what they want! For them, it is a determined effort: they want company and they will choose who it will be. These women don't wait around and hope someone will choose them. Many have taken the initiative and taken over the selection process!

Remember, we are the generation who devoured books like *Sex and the Single Girl* (1962) by Helen Gurley Brown; *The Joy of Sex* (1972) by Alex Comfort; and Germaine Greer's *The Female Eunuch* (1970). Along with the sealed section in *Cleo* magazines, books like these defined a new enlightened sexuality for women and sparked the feminist movement. Attitudes to sex became more liberated, the Pill gave us options, and taboo subjects were out in the open. And we were there! Let's not forget that.

*****

I recently visited Cleo, a very special girlfriend in Bali. She has lived there for many years, after opting out of a fast-paced corporate life and building her own villa overlooking the vast expanses of the Indian Ocean. She then set up a very successful restaurant in a northern Balinese village.

Cleo was talking with me about my progress with this book, and asked me, 'Chris, have you written that every women should have a Caesar?'

I was confused, so she continued, 'Well, women of our age have every right to a healthy sex life, but many times we are disappointed in our partners – or we haven't been lucky enough to find a gorgeous man – so we need to take care of ourselves.'

Yes, we do know that regular sex keeps us healthy:

- It raises our levels of immunoglobulin to improve immunity.
- We are less likely to develop heart disease.
- Our blood pressure is lowered with sexual activity.
- It is a form of exercise, which is essential to our health.
- It releases pain-reducing hormones and can relieve back and leg pain, menstrual cramps, arthritis and headaches.
- It improves sleep.
- It is a relief from stress.
- It improves bladder control.

Cleo's sound advice then is to have our own battery-operated Caesar, which will allow us to be in control of our own sexual activities in the comfort of our own home.

If you have never tried this, read on, because you might be fascinated (as I was) to see that many women do!

When I returned home from my trip to visit Cleo in Bali, I attended our next Sixties Meetup event. It was a large group, split up into smaller tables. I was sitting at one when one hilarious member of the group began talking about sexual encounters and soon blurted out the question, 'Has everyone got a Bob?'

Many of us frowned, asking 'A who?' to which she replied, 'A battery-operated boyfriend!' We all laughed so much, and were so surprised because many ladies said they did!

This session was a bit of a revelation and left me thinking that I had some exploring to do in this area if I am to really become a fully self-actualised woman in her sixties!

So, I decided that one of these gadgets was a 'must have' and set about finding one!

With head held high and shoulders back, I strode into a local sex shop trying to look nonchalant. Believe me, walking into a bar to meet a man from a dating site was nothing compared to this! What if someone I knew saw me? Trying to ignore the mind-boggling array of titillating sex objects on every shelf, I eventually found a terrifying-looking selection of vibrators. My eventual research list included:

- Lipstick Vibe Bullet Vibrator – discreet in your handbag
- Purple Passion Mini Waterproof Vibrator – a royal colour
- The JimmyJane Iconic Bullet – perfect for beginners
- The Gigi – I believe it is like a stylish USB
- The Rabbit – popular after its *Sex and the City* moment

Obviously I could not then ignore the fact that this section had to be included in this book. After all, a healthy libido is our own responsibility!

Happy hunting ladies, and I hope this encouragement brings you renewed confidence and pleasure in your personal life. Of course, ordering online would be so less stressful!

Get out there and create adventures for yourself, and remain interesting. Online connections allow us all to do this so easily, but we must be sensible and realistic, knowing we have to be in charge. Whether you connect through online dating sites, Meetup groups, local community centres, or personal invitation, just do it and meet with more people.

****

CHAPTER 11

The Active Brain:
Keep Learning

In my 50s, I was given an art class as a birthday present. Despite feeling somewhat devoid of artistic ability, I was excited that I was getting involved with something out of my comfort zone. Everyone else in the group seemed to have a degree of skill, and although we had to wear a dramatic hat, colourful clothes and bring a bottle of wine to enjoy, I soon learned that I had little artistic talent! However, I met some feisty women, laughed a lot and took home a completed art piece which to this day I have not shared with anyone!

Learning new things at any age opens up new worlds. Putting yourself out of your comfort zone stimulates the brain, allows you to appreciate the expertise of other people and puts you in a situation where you might make new friends.

One of the joys of our sixties is that we probably have the time and freedom to choose new things to investigate and dabble in, or even master – and our minds are far more capable than we realise. We probably don't have to do the latest business courses to stay competitive and up to date (although that could be interesting and useful). It's time to break loose and branch out!

The capacity to learn is a gift
The ability to learn is a skill
The willingness to learn is a choice

—Brian Herbert

Apart from the health benefits of exercise, learning a sporting activity at our age with little or no competitive pressure, adds an element of social connectivity and fun. Be it golf, tennis, netball, swimming, walking or cycling, a sport gets you into an active community and helps to keep the body and brain alert and healthy.

Libraries offer courses in a wide number of subject areas, not just the more traditional ones we learned in school. You can learn about the science of cooking, new discoveries involving our brains, memory, and self-healing. You can study astrology, gazing at the stars through telescopes from the comfort of your own home. Websites such as www.udemy.com, www.courseca.com, and mooc.org are gateways to some fascinating online courses that are inexpensive and convenient. The subject matter is endless.

The Internet has made all of this possible. Through this amazing medium we sixty-year-olds can reinvent ourselves. We have access to news, discoveries, history and geography, the arts, science, drama, famous people, stories, movies and so much more. YouTube in itself can entertain you every evening with old movies, meaningful speeches, funny clips and sales presentations. You can sign up to online courses about every subject matter imaginable. The Internet is an open window to the world, so if you haven't yet got yourself an iPhone and iPad, you are missing out big time!

I recently met Kate, aged 61 and just retired. She had been on the corporate ladder all her working life, with huge responsibilities for banks, charities and the board of her children's school. Understandably, she was feeling quite lost. On top of that, she had separated from her husband (still remaining friends) and moved to live by the beach. How daunting to have her daily routine, corporate responsibilities and generous income end, even though she was probably financially secure. Kate came along to one of my Meetup groups and was astounded to hear so many opportunities for involvement from the other women. She was eager to enroll in a practical language course, attend talks at the local library and join the Friend's Group at the local arts centre. There are so many possibilities when you don't have a nine-to-five job!

When you stop learning
you stop growing.
Don't be
at the same place next year
as you are now.

—Joel Osteen

We know that technology cannot replace human contact and real-time experience. There is still so much pleasure in curling up with a good book, playing a board game with grandchildren, or shopping in a real store. We may not be as tech-savvy as our kids or grandkids, but we can gain enormous benefit from technology. Dive in and give it a go. It is an indulgence you can switch on anywhere – in a café, waiting for a train or plane, or travelling solo. You can:

- Read newspapers and magazines online
- Watch the news
- Email your friends and family
- Join groups to play games, discuss topics of interest or organise to meet
- Learn a language
- Learn how to play an instrument
- Buy stocks and shares or trade on the financial markets (firstly seeking professional advice)
- Connect to www.ted.com to listen to influential people speaking skillfully to the world
- Sign up to a course
- Find fascinating podcasts
- Find the meaning of anything and everything!

I spend many hours researching about the brain, the third eye, numerology, our memory, global women's groups and neuroscience.

I love connecting to www.ted.com to listen to inspirational talks by the likes of Jane Fonda, JK Rowling, Richard Branson and the most watched of all, Sir Ken Robinson. Other brilliant scientists, doctors,

The Internet is becoming
the Town Square
for the Global Village
of tomorrow.

—Bill Gates

artists and humanitarians share their remarkable stories and are accessible to us whenever and wherever it suits!

We can bring art galleries, museums, space, travel and entertainment into our homes so easily through our digital devices. This remarkable invention gives us life-long access to learning of our choice.

Download game apps and play bridge, mahjong, scrabble and many more games either on your own, with family members, or in a group – an interesting concept with team members or opponents all over the world.

There is unfortunately a dark side to the Internet as well. There are many people who like to lurk in the dark and prey on our natural instinct to trust people – and they are very good at finding a vulnerability and taking advantage.

Be careful, ask others you know and trust for their opinion, and if a deal or a person sound too good to be true, they probably are. Be scam aware by following these simple tips:

- Official organisations such as government departments, communication companies and utility companies will never ask for personal information by phone
- Never give out personal details over the phone to anyone (unless a trusted person)

- Never give permission for your computer to be taken over
- Always sign up to reputable sites
- If you suspect a scam caller, ask for their name and a contact number and call back to authenticate the caller
- Delete obvious scam emails immediately and report them
- Refer to www.snopes.com to check whether a supposed fact or rumour online is actually true
- Be aware of 'love scams' which are proliferating on a growing number of Internet dating sites. Cunning, dishonest crooks and syndicates use fake photographs and false data, and prey on older, vulnerable people, evidenced by so many heartbreaking stories of how genuine, innocent people have been sucked in. Never, ever give money to anyone you have only ever met online!

I have a laptop, an iPad, an iPhone, and an iWatch. All these amazing devices connect with each other, minimising the risk of me losing data. I have an external backup downloaded with all my computer information, plus everything is saved in 'the cloud', which is an online data centre providing extra security. I learned to do this the hard way after once losing years of photos.

To personalise my digital experience and to have a bit of fun, I own:

- A trendy bag on wheels
- A shoulder bag (a free duty free liquor bag)

- An iPad case to prop up the machine
- A charger which fits onto my iPhone, allowing me extended power
- Blue earphones (so cool)

Many tech stores around the world offer amazing benefits once you are a customer. You become a member with access to free classes either online or in their stores. Apart from being trendy, friendly and accommodating, it's really easy. I love joining these in-store groups to learn new ideas, functions or gadget upgrades in the company of similarly aged people, couples and singles, who are also really interested in learning. It is such fun to interact with others and not worry about asking dumb questions, as we are all in the same boat, and eager to learn.

When travelling, the Internet becomes your companion, keeping you abreast of the latest news and connecting you with family and friends. When sightseeing, just find a café or beautiful spot, get connected and share it with someone back home. This adds to the joy of travel. Through the Internet you can keep learning, train your memory, find out anything and everything, and keep up with the younger generation. Just dive in!

Live as if you are to die tomorrow
Learn as if you are to live forever.

—Ghandi

CHAPTER 12

The Power Plan

Congratulations! You have now arrived at the most important part of this book dedicated to helping you make your sixties your best decade ever. Life can be exciting and fulfilling if you have the courage to shape it the way you want.

Do you still have lists of things you want to accomplish – or can you be content with your life the way it is?

It's time now to get organised for real action and transformational results by creating your individual plan. The question to ask yourself is: Where do I see myself in ten years? Whether you are in your early, middle or late sixties, you can start now with your 10-year plan.

In Chapter 3 I introduced you to the exercise 'My Circle of Life', where you recorded your life accomplishments so far, and identified things you want to pursue in the next decade.

I suggest you review that one more time, and possibly update it now that you have progressed to this point: you may have more ideas to add.

By now you will be more eager and excited than ever to give it all a go and I have just the tool to make it happen!

Introducing The Mega To-Do List:

    ✓ It is the ultimate, all-encompassing power tool.
    ✓ This is not any old to-do list.
    ✓ This is something on a different level.
    ✓ It is simple and enjoyable but it has to be active to be effective!

'When you don't have a vision
or a plan for the future,
your mind has no choice
but to dwell in the past.

—Dr Steve Maraboli

The Mega To-Do List can help you achieve multiple outcomes: It can be the key to focussing your energies on creating your highest quality of time.

It can resolve or relieve loneliness by helping you decide if you really do want to share your life with others, or be content by yourself.

It can improve your relationships with your children, family members and friends.

It can inspire you to get involved in your community and to learn new things.

It is your power tool to developing a decade of intention.

It keeps you accountable.

Once started, it can evolve to be powerful and exciting.

The trouble with not having a goal
is that you can spend your life
running up and down the field
and never score.

—Bill Copeland

Don't wait for the beginning of a year or month to start this, do it right now – the power of now is important. When created, your Mega To-Do-List has intention. Dreams become possibilities and possibilities become real opportunities. It's a plan of action: nothing is forgotten or overlooked.

Why do it? Because research proves that people who write down their intentions have a much higher success rate than those who don't.

Your Mega To-Do List is your:

– Mind organiser
– Memory jogger
– Creative path
– 'I wish I could' list
– Back-up plan
– Dare list
– Social connector
– 'What if' dreamer
– Must-try list
– Books to read
– Movies to watch
– Exercise schedule
– Recipes to try
– Courses to enroll in
– New hobbies and skills to learn
– Travel organiser
– Estate planning/Will structure
– Financial health check
– Friends to meet
– Planner (hour, day, week, month, year)

Ten years is exactly
120 months
520 weeks
3650 days ... it's not a lot!

Planning Your Own Mega To-Do List

We all achieve in different ways, and a wonderful thing about this age is that we usually know ourselves very well. It is important to embrace the techniques that best motivate you to succeed whenever you try something new.

Consider what type of sensory person you are and how you might enhance the creation of your To-Do List.

Visual stimulation works for me as I love colours, pictures and doodles. I use bright post-it notes of various shapes and sizes, and cut pictures out of magazines as illustrations, reminders and decoration.

You can embrace the sense of **smell to create** a calming atmosphere by burning natural aromatic oils or candles whilst working on your Mega To-Do List.

If you are a tactile person and love **touching** then you may want to include ribbon, wrapping paper and natural materials such as wood to bind your To-Do sheets. You might create a cover, a bookmark, or buy stickers to make the process appealing to you.

Appeal to your **sense of taste** by including recipes, new restaurants, and the cuisine you will enjoy during visits to other countries in your To-Do List.

And of course music - **listen** to motivating songs or calming music as you create your To-Do List and allow yourself to imagine what is possible.

Then the sixth sense of **intuition** may manifest itself in a creative space: the kitchen, the garden, a café, library or somewhere special – or in your dreams and imagination.

I choose to keep my Mega To-Do List in my laptop case, or inside my diary. I have on hand highlighters, coloured pens and a pencil. I use shapes – circles, rectangles, triangles – and have a paper bag with cut-out flowers, quotes, expressions and images of the odd car/plane/house/holiday, just in case!

Finding the best time to work on your list is an individual choice – maybe at the same time each day or the last thing before bed. Whatever time is best for you, reflect on your day, move forward any task not completed, then set intentions for the following day. Maybe you just 'fly by the seat of your pants' and grab whatever time is available, or as your mood suits. Remember that if you set times and deadlines, you will avoid procrastination!

A properly designed and executed Mega To-Do List will:

- Avoid wasting time
- Give you an intention
- Ensure you do what's important to you
- Help you get more done in a day/a week

- Reduce anxiety and stress
- Allocate deadlines

Try to manage your Mega To-Do List to keep it under control. If there are too many diverse tasks, then you may find it too difficult. Gather together similar tasks and allocate an indicative timeframe to work on the list, say half-an-hour or one hour at a time to keep it realistic and focused.

An active in-motion Mega To-Do List can be a reflection of so many actions, thoughts, mood swings, celebrations and more. If you miss planning or recording for a couple of days, put in a reason why.

Now, let's create this masterpiece of intention …

I have created a template with options, for you to download and print. You can create a weekly, monthly or a whole 52-week To-Do List, as well as your own cover, or have it bound. Put it in a place where you can see the creation evolve.

Go to www.powerofwomeninoursixties.com to download the template.

I suggest you print a few copies – I've seen it done as a concertina.

If a task is not done on a specific day, it is moved on one day or one week – or even a month. For example, I have had 'clean the carpet' in my list for a few weeks.

Look back at your Circle of Life too. You may choose to select some of the things you wanted to do more with, and add them to your To-do List. You then accomplish them, move them, or delete them – the list is not stagnant. It moves with your energy and time.

So, let's get down to it. The Mega To-Do List for Women in their Sixties is about to be your reality, and will ensure that this decade contains goals and activities of great value … one week at a time!

Make your Mega To-Do List your new best friend! It can be adapted and included in an everyday, ordinary hands-on diary, an online diary – or you can use my template.

Mega To-do List

Week / Month

Monday	Tuesday	Wednesday	Thursday

Thoughts written down can become a reality

Power of Women
in Our SIXTIES

LIFE & STYLE FOR MODERN WOMEN IN OUR SIXTIES

_ear

Friday	Saturday	Sunday	Notes

I was once asked to create a picture, like a vision board, depicting where I saw myself in ten years. I collected lots of pictures with energy and colour, and words with strong messages, and began to compile my picture. This took me a few days, at coffee time, wine time and bedtime! The end result made me feel extraordinary.

It was my vision of happiness and contentment, and I could feel the good energy it exuded. The best thing was that I knew it was possible to achieve. Working towards my vision would be a personal project that I would really enjoy. Having a visual representation of my desires as a focus each day fills me with anticipation and excitement about the journey ahead.

Now that you have read this book and you are equipped with your Mega To-Do List, let's explore the opportunities ahead.

Because of the many incredible women I have met at this stage in life, I know anything is possible: but the thing that stands out is the power of support and togetherness when women unite.

The power of women in their sixties is a force to reckon with. We have ten years to liberate and reinvent ourselves, so let's choose to become a driving force with power rather than retreating meekly and disappearing into invisibility.

By recording your dreams
and goals on paper,
you set in motion the process
of becoming the person
you most want to be.
Put your future in good
hands—your own.

—Mark Victor Hansen

Our power is our experience – strong thoughts, strong body, strong will, moving forward. We have the power to change the world for good, based on our sixty-plus years of lived experience.

Let's go a step further in our sixties, and instead of organically forming friendships and support groups, actively go out there and organise them.

Today's world is a complex one and with our experience, we are more than qualified to gather, support each other, and become a force for positive change in the world.

When women support each other, incredible things happen.

—Anonymous

CONCLUSION

Embrace the best decade of your life – your sixties – and realise that there is a sense of urgency. It passes quickly. Create quality of time and expand your world. This really is the best time ever to be sixty! We are fortunate. Of course the good times do not end when we reach seventy, but don't put off the good times until then.

Do it now!

I hope you have enjoyed reading this book as much as I have enjoyed writing it. I have shared many of my life experiences as I approached sixty, and now during my sixties. I have also shared stories from so many incredible women at my Power of Sixty Year old Women Meetup groups. I hope that their stories of courage, resilience and hope also inspire you to believe that you can be and do anything you want in your sixties, regardless of your earlier experiences.

Life can be exciting and fulfilling in your sixties if you have the courage to shape it the way you want. Together, I believe we have the power to change not only our own lives, but the lives of other women, and the world, by supporting good causes.

Who knows, our example could inspire our daughters and granddaughters to continue our legacy and become future torch bearers for the Power of Sixty Year Old Women when they reach their time as well.

I would love your feedback on this book. Please feel free to contact me at:

www.powerofwomeninoursixties.com

thepowerofwomeninoursixties@gmail.com

The woman I was yesterday introduced me to the woman I am today; which makes me very excited about meeting the woman I will become tomorrow.

—Uknown

RECOMMENDED READING

Reinvented Lives
by
Elizabeth & Charles Handy

Chocolate for a Woman's Soul
by
Kay Allenbaugh

Living Alone & Loving It
by
Barbara Feldon

Secrets of Six-Figure Women
by
Barbara Stanny

The Age Well Project
by
Annabel Streets & Susan Saunders

Brain Rules for Ageing Well
by
Jon Medina

Live the Life you Love And Stop Getting By
by
Barbara Sher

Smart Women Publish
by
Bev Ryan

In your Prime
by
India Knight

Badass Mums
by
Sarah Firth

Sixty Summers
by
Amanda Hampson

Set Yourself Free in Relationships
by
Shirley Smith

The Most Powerful Woman in the Room is You
by
Lydia Fenet

Keep Marching
by
Kristin Rowe-Finkbeiner

200 Women
by
Geoff Blackwell & Ruth Hobday

The Second Half of Your Life
by
Jill Shaw Ruddock

Avoid Retirement & Stay Alive
by
David Bogan & Keith Davies

Live the Life you Love And Stop Just Getting By
by
Barbara Sher

Trust Your Senses
by
Deb Lange

The Ways Women Age
by
Abigail T Brookes

Celebrating the Older You
by
Jo Schlehofer

04143622-00928073

Printed in the United States
By Bookmasters